The
That Is Loved
Never Forgets

Recovering from Loss:

When Humans

and Animals

Lose Their

Companions

KAETHERYN WALKER

Illustrations by Jeannine Ann

Healing Arts Press
Rochester, Vermont

Healing Arts Press
One Park Street
Rochester, Vermont 05767

Healing Arts Press is a division of Inner Traditions International
www.InnerTraditions.com

Note to the reader: This book is intended as an informational guide. The remedies, approaches, and techniques described herein are meant to supplement, and not to be a substitute for, professional veterinary care or treatment. They should not be used to treat a serious ailment without prior consultation with a state-licensed veterinarian.

Library of Congress Cataloging-in-Publication Data
Walker, Kaetheryn, 1956–
    The heart that is loved never forgets : recovering from loss : when humans and animals
  lose their companions / Kaetheryn Walker.
       p.   cm.
  Includes bibliographical references.
  ISBN 0-89281-702-X (pbk. : alk. paper)
    1. Pet owners—Psychology. 2. Pets—Death—Psychological aspects.
  3. Bereavement—Psychological aspects. 4. Grief in animals. 5. Human-animal
  relationships. 6. Homeopathic veterinary medicine. I. Title.
  SF411.47.W325 1998
  155.9'37—dc21   98-12366
                                              CIP

Printed and bound in the United States

10 9 8 7 6 5 4 3 2 1

Text design and layout by Rachel Goldenberg
This book was typeset in Garamond with Wade Sans Light as the display typeface

Grieve not,
nor speak of me with tears,
but laugh and talk of me
as if I were beside you . . .
I loved you so—
'twas Heaven here with you.

Isla Paschal Richardson

Old Friends

*In winter, when the cold winds blow to rattle the
barn doors, There is calm within, a quiet munching
of hay as
Snowflakes beat themselves against windowpanes.
Adjusting blankets, I find that soft, velvety place high
on the inside of a hind leg,
Its warmth thawing numbed fingers.*

*At dawn, when the light strikes the top of the old pine
tree, I am greeted by soft nickers, anticipation of
breakfast.
On venturing into the stillness of morning and the
warming sunlight,
Hooves crunch through newly drifted snow. One
stands immobile, a statue, watching,
Listening, breath rising in crystalline clouds that drift
away to snow somewhere else.*

*In spring, when the snows have gone and the ground
given up its frost,
They lie stretched out, bones warmed by strengthening
sun,
Reminiscent of beached whales.
I move quietly among them, checking for signs of life,
humbled by the trust that lets me
Touch a face cradled by warm earth.*

*On soft, summer nights, they become different
creatures,
No longer the friends I know by day. More wary, less
trusting, they melt silently into
Woods, if approached too boldly, surfacing once more
in unexpected places.*

I keep my distance, and watch as they graze in a
Mist lit by fireflies and moonlight.

With the first cool winds that mark the beginning of
the end of summer,
There is a quickening of blood. They run in exultation,
great strides that shake the earth,
Giving expression to that fire still burning inside.
I shout with joy, honored to be witness to the
Beauty of their movement.

In fall, we walk through woods where once we
galloped, as
Shards of sunlight filter through trees, the path a
kaleidoscope of fallen leaves,
Red, yellow, green and gold. Listening and watching,
We drink in the fullness of life around us.
Companions at peace with one another.

There are only three now, one black, one brown, one
with stars on his sides.
They know the best of me, the worst of me, and love
me nonetheless.
I cherish each moment, wrinkled nostrils as they
drink,
The clean smell of their breath, the rub of a head on
my shoulder.
I would not trade these quiet joys. They mark the
rhythm of my life.

Each evening, before I leave the barn,
I speak my incantation for protection till the dawn.
Good night. Sleep well. Be well.
I love you.
Old friends.

Nena Norton

Contents

A Brief Introduction to Homeopathy

While this book mentions how we, as humans, grieve the loss of our animal companions and can heal from our emotional losses, it primarily addresses these topics in relation to our animal companions. It often goes on to discuss using homeopathic remedies as aids to emotional healing for these animals.

In the United States the use of homeopathy as a complementary aid for healing physical illness in both humans and animals is gaining widespread recognition. In 1982 Veterinarian Richard Pitcairn first published his book *Natural Health for Dogs and Cats,* a revised edition of which has been subsequently published by Rodale Press. Dr. Pitcairn was among the first to address such topics as feeding animals a natural diet, grieving the loss of an animal companion, and using herbs, nutrition, and homeopathic remedies to aid animal healing. He was also an early voice of concern about the possible harmful effects of vaccinations on animals' immune systems.

Concurrent with the use of homeopathic remedies for physical illness is the understanding that homeopathic remedies also may be used as aids in healing emotional traumas. There has also been a recent upsurge in evidence that, like humans, animals possess an emotional life, including the ability to experience painful emotions and their ill effects. Following this recognition, a natural next step is to use homeopathic remedies for healing emotional symptoms in animals.

This may seem like a novel idea to many people, but it is not a new theory in veterinary practice. Christopher Day, a noteworthy British veterinarian, has been using homeopathic medicine in his rural practice since 1972. His excellent book *The Homoeopathic Treatment of Small Animals: Principles and Practice* was first published by India's B. Jain Publishers in 1985. I have found it to be the most valuable and accurate text in my entire library of books on the topic of veterinary homeopathy. It was in this small, rather innocuous-looking paperback that I first read about emotional trauma in animals and which remedies are most effective for treating them.

In the following pages of this book I attempt to illustrate, by way of accounts of my own animals, how animals may express emotional traumas and how I have helped them heal emotionally. I make reference to a variety of homeopathic remedies and their indications for use, but for a more detailed explanation of how homeopathic remedies work, indications of positive responses, remedy and potency selection, guidelines to dosage frequency, and when to call the vet, please refer to my book *Homeopathic First Aid for Animals.*

When using homeopathic remedies to relieve emotional trauma in animals, several points should be clearly understood before beginning. First, it would be foolhardy to overlook the possibility that a physical ailment is causing an emotional symptom in an animal. It is vital to have a qualified veterinarian rule out a physical condition before assuming that the roots of a problem lie in the emotional realm. For example, many cats who are experiencing urinary tract problems will void outside the litter tray in unacceptable places. Rather than being an aberrant mental symptom, this is a visible plea for help. Cats will often urinate over bathtub or shower drains, as cool air in the drain helps relieve the burning symptoms that often accompany urinary tract problems. In such a case, to delay medical treatment because the physical problem was mistaken for an emotional one might jeopardize the life of the cat. Do seek out the professional advice of a licensed veterinarian, and never assume anything.

Second, some animal behaviors are intrinsic to a specific species. In other words, animals may not always respond to a given situation in ways that humans clearly understand. Animals within a herd, pack, pride, or school will each respond in harmony with their position within the social structure of that particular grouping. It is therefore important to fully understand the nuances and particulars of behavior of the species of animal you are interacting with.

One woman I know used homeopathic remedies to try to alter her older cat's aggressive responses when she adopted more cats. What she did not consider was that her cat was simply exhibiting a normal feline response to having to share territory with several new members. The cat did, indeed, become more mellow when treated with several remedies used to modify her behavior, but she was no longer her usual, happy self. Because she was not really suffering from a true emotional trauma, there was nothing to be healed from; the remedies only changed her essence—her true nature—and wrought change where none was necessary. This is a clear example of why not to tamper with the harmonious design of Nature. Subsequently, the woman stopped using homeopathic remedies to alter her cat's behavior, and to all our great relief several weeks of very natural, catlike infighting occurred, during which the ranks of order were well established and the original, resident cat reigned supreme.

Many professionals are available to answer questions and help the public understand the normal behaviors of specific species. Your veterinarian is always a good choice, and also consider dog obedience instructors and horse trainers. Don't forget professional groomers, kennel and cattery operators, breeder organizations, pet store owners, shelter workers, dairy, sheep and goat farmers, and animal technicians. These are all people who work with animals on a daily basis and are very familiar with the type they interact with.

In appendix 2 I also make reference to many good books on the topic of animal behavior that are available. Reference books, also available at libraries, list books by topic, and these can be a wealth of information about texts, periodicals, and magazines that are out of general circulation but can be very informative.

Homeopathic remedies are renowned for healing symptoms unique to the individual. Although two people may have the same cold virus, each person's immune system will respond differently, and will benefit from different homeopathic remedies. One person's stuffy head, dry mouth, and bland nasal discharges may respond to the remedy Pulsatilla. Another person's chilliness, wet sneezes, and sore throat may respond to the remedy Silicea.

Using homeopathic remedies for emotional healing works on the same principle. Just as no two individuals respond in the same way to a common physical stressor, no two individuals will respond quite the same way to a common emotional stressor. Two dogs living in the same household may each experience fear triggered by the same stimuli, yet exhibit different symptoms. One dog who is frightened of going to the vet may become totally wild and violent, a situation where the remedy Aconite would be of great benefit. Another dog may demonstrate his fear by trembling, crouching into as small a space as possible, and urinating or defecating uncontrollably; this is a situation where the remedy Gelsemium would be of great benefit. As you will see, each of the homeopathic remedies mentioned in this book are used to help heal very specific emotional symptoms.

Edward Bach, the English physician who developed the Bach Flower Essences, believed that there are levels of disease. He believed that all disease manifests on the psychic, emotional, and physical levels of the individual. He also believed that all disease begins with psychic trauma and evolves, if left untreated, to deeper and more irreversible displays of the body crying for help. He noted in his patients that psychic trauma occurred first; if left untreated, psychic symptoms developed into mental symptoms; and if mental symptoms were left untreated, they would develop into physical symptoms. Dr. Bach believed that by the time his patients manifested physical symptoms of disease, they were in the end-stages of disease and their symptoms were harder to treat.

Homeopathic remedies are available in different strengths, or potencies. The potency of a remedy dictates its use in resolving the symptoms of the different levels of disease that Dr. Bach wrote and lectured about. Lower potencies from 3c to 30c are generally used for localized physical symptoms; they work on the cellular and organ level of illness. Higher potencies of 200c to 1m are what I call midrange remedies that work primarily on emotions like fear, resentment, and depression. Very high potencies, from 10m to CM, work at the psychic level; symptoms that are termed psychic are those such as seeing things that aren't there, imaginary smells, and other delusional states.

Humans and animals experience two types of symptoms, subjective and objective. Subjective symptoms are those known only to an individual, unless described via spoken language to another person. Pain is an example of a subjective symptom. Objective symptoms are observable, such as photophobia (eye sensitivity to bright light, such as squinting in sunlight) or vomiting after eating.

Because we cannot know when an animal is experiencing subjective symptoms such as delusional states, it is difficult for most people to work with animals at the psychic level of disease. We can, however, use homeopathic remedies to work with animals on an emotional level because we can observe actions and reactions that indicate that an emotion is being experienced. The previous example of fear of going to the vet is a good example of actions that indicate a specific emotional state.

The time at which a dose "wears off," or no longer is assisting healing and needs to be repeated, varies with each individual. All individuals get well at their own rate of healing. Some homeopaths believe that it takes an individual as long to get well as it did for that individual to become ill.

The duration of all single doses of remedies, regardless of potency, depends upon whether the symptoms are acute or chronic. With acute symptoms, the body tends to use up the beneficial action of a single dose of a remedy fairly quickly. Extremely acute symptoms, such as severe bleeding or terror, require repeating doses as frequently as every half hour. Less acute symptoms, such as a sprain or a slight fright, require repeating doses two to four times a day. With chronic symptoms, the body tends to use up the beneficial healing action of a single dose of a remedy much less quickly. One to six weeks may lapse before symptoms return and a subsequent dose needs to be given. Chronic symptoms may evolve from untreated (or badly managed) acute symptoms: an old hip injury that develops into joint stiffness and lameness or extreme panic during a thunderstorm that later develops into a nervous, high-strung nature.

When working with animals, we can be sure that it is time to repeat a remedy when we see observable symptoms return. If symptoms do not return it is unwise to repeat a remedy, because remedies will induce the symptoms if they are not already present. In the words of the famous homeopath James Tyler Kent, "Go fast slowly." He was adamant in his instruction to not only use the right remedy in the right potency, but not to repeat the remedy until the last dose had done its work.

There are many examples in the following pages of how homeopathy helped animals to heal from a variety of emotional traumas stemming from grief. You will learn how remedies were chosen for the different animals in the stories ahead, and how the remedies were given over several days, weeks, or months. Some of the animals you meet in these pages were treated with homeopathy because there was no other option available; vets had no answers, and animal psychologists are rare in Maine, where I live. Others of these animals were treated with homeopathy because I felt strongly that homeopathy was the only healing modality that would truly heal them. All are real animals, though some, like Hervena the rabbit, have gone on to graze other pastures.

Lastly, potencies of 200c to 1m and up are not always available at the corner health food store. They may have to be ordered from a homeopathic pharmacy or distributor, but your local health food store can be a good resource for finding a distributor of higher-potency remedies.

Professional practitioners of animal homeopathy who are certain they have chosen the right remedy *for the right reason* will use higher potencies with confidence. This is not a task to be taken lightly by the layperson. If you are not sure what you are doing, please, for the well-being of your animal companion, seek the advice of a professional who is experienced in treating animals with homeopathic remedies. Your role, as you work with a professional, will be to monitor responses, take notes on your animal's progress, and provide emotional and environmental support as your animal heals. Without your good nursing care, the homeopath's work would be only half done! Assisting their animal companions through the process of emotional healing is enough of a task for most people who are new to the use of homeopathy without trying to also figure out what remedy to use, what potency to use, and how often to repeat it.

In summation, I would like to encourage you to listen to your animal companion. You are your animal's liaison to the world, providing protection and participating in a two-way interpretation of events and responses, and no one knows him or her better than you do. Follow your intuition and your heart, and know that you were chosen for this very special role in your animal's brief stay here in the world. But in all things please be sure that what you are doing is right. After all, the animal who loves you is counting on you to make all the right choices.

Introduction

As we near the close of the twentieth century and enter a new millennium, humans in record numbers are becoming increasingly concerned with the well-being and destiny of the multitude of nonhuman species with whom we share our fragile planet. The evening news brings many accounts of the animals in our world: groups of people gather together to free whales trapped under sheets of ice or beached in shallow tidal pools; dolphins and sea turtles are rescued from extreme, life-threatening situations; and thousands of seabirds, otters, and seals are saved from disastrous oil spills. Of land-bound creatures, we hear about eagle nests being safely removed from construction sites and relocated to protected habitat, and gray wolf relocation projects designed to reintroduce wild species to national forest lands.

Worldwide organizations, such as the Fund for Animals, International Fund for Animal Welfare, and Greenpeace, have been founded to protect the rights of animals on a global scale. In America, organizations such as the Progressive Animal Welfare Society and the Animal Legal Defense Fund, both of which represent animals' legal rights, and the Association of Veterinarians for

Animal Rights have been founded only in the last twenty years. And there is a growing trend to reverse the long-held concept that nondomestic animals are pests and that their impact on human habitats requires extensive animal damage control programs (at a cost of $30 million annually). Instead, wildlife and their symbiotic relationship to the ecosystems of planet Earth have become a priority on which, many naturalists and biologists agree, our own fate may be inexorably linked.

Even the creatures who share our lives and homes seem to be in the spotlight. Firefighters rush cats and dogs from burning buildings; a community effort pulls a stranded horse from a pond; and lost companion animals are returned to their anxious families hundreds of miles away. Countless organizations now work for the welfare and humane treatment of the animal companions in our lives. Those more well-known include the Humane Society of the United States and the American Society for the Prevention of Cruelty to Animals.[1]

In addition, concern for the health and emotional well-being of our nonhuman companions is on the rise. New well-health maintenance and illness modalities that serve the physical needs of companion animals are becoming more widely available. Homeopathy, Reiki, chiropractic, massage, and acupuncture are eagerly sought out by people for their animal companions. These types of complementary health care services are thriving and represent a growing awareness in the general population that animals are more than mere physical entities, whose ills and health needs can be adequately addressed by the application of chemical drugs and surgical solutions.

From their own experiences and observations, people know that the animals in their lives do respond to touch, to love, and are capable of experiencing a full range of emotions from happiness to grief. Instead of merely caring for the physical needs of companion animals, many people are seeking animal health care services that foster their companion animals' emotional, mental, and spiritual health.

Many individuals believe that their animal companions are not only cognitive beings but capable of communicating with and understanding their human counterparts on very subtle levels.[2] Such services as those offered by animal communicators are now widely available and enthusiastically sought out. These practitioners of psychic animal communication do not need to have previously met or even to be in the presence of an animal to communicate with him or her. They accomplish their task through the application of the theory that all beings are interconnected, and access to any individual is achieved by tapping into what is referred to as the Universal Energy or Universal Consciousness.

Animal psychics not only assist people in finding lost or stolen animals, but can also evaluate, from a remote location, the physical condition of an animal's body.[3] After making initial contact with an animal, an animal psychic will ask the animal for permission to "go inside its body" to find areas of pain or discomfort. Once such an assessment is made, revealing symptoms that may have otherwise gone undetected, the information can be relayed to a practitioner, such as an animal homeopathic practitioner, for whom such subjective symptoms as tightness, or burning sensations, can be a revealing piece of information that can lead to the correct selection of a homeopathic remedy or to an adjunct therapy such as chiropractic or massage.

Many people who live with animals are convinced that they also experience a full range of emotions; emotions such as grief, rage, and jealousy, which not long ago were thought to be limited to the human realm of experience. Many veterinarians are now aware of the use of flower essences and homeopathic remedies as aids to emotional healing for animals, and offer them to their clients.

Since Elisabeth Kübler-Ross's *On Death and Dying* was published, there has been much attention given to the process of death and its aftermath, the grieving process.[4] What has, until recently, been ignored in the American culture is both the grief a person experiences when their animal companion dies and the grief an animal may experience when another animal within a family group dies. Numerous organizations now offer meetings for members to discuss the process of grieving. People now openly discuss their experience of losing an animal companion, and others talk about being with a beloved animal companion as he or she undergoes a natural or assisted death process. Even the College of Veterinary Medicine at Michigan State University offers a pet loss support hotline where people coping with the loss of an animal companion can speak with veterinary students trained by a professional grief counselor.[5]

Despite our evolutionary gains, the human species is under siege.

Overwhelmed by crowded urban centers, we reel from an explosion of technological information and lifestyles that leave us all frazzled and overwrought from a lack of time to recreate, unwind, and mentally and emotionally process the avalanche of information and experiences that fill our every waking moment. What keeps many people in balance and provides a focused, simple meaning to their hectic existence are the unrestrained, satisfying, and sincere relationships that they experience with their animal companions. These relationships are not overshadowed by the social limitations that so commonly accompany our other daily interactions. With the animals we share our lives with, we are unfettered by human rules of conduct and are free to explore the intricacies of mutual respect and symbiotic coevolution. And if we are capable of being quiet enough, compassionate enough, honest enough, and courageous enough to see, we are blessed through their reflection of our true selves and begin to understand—and accept—our own essences, frailties, and strengths. Since the death of one of my greatest friends, a cat named McTavish, many people have approached me to talk about their own animal companions' illnesses and death processes. It was part of my healing process to walk with them through their journeys. Hearing that their grief was as profound for their animal companions as mine had been for McTavish jolted me out of my isolated arrogance that no one had ever grieved as deeply for an animal as I had for him. I have come to understand that all of us suffer when we lose a friend. That the friend is of another species has no bearing on the depth or the reach of our grief, nor does the species of one who grieves matter.

In these pages I share what I have learned and observed and what my animal companions have taught me. To them, my animal friends, I owe a great debt of gratitude. I hope that you, dear reader, will find solace and comfort in these pages. I write it for you, with deep love and compassion for your loss and your courage. Grief and the rewards of healing are journeys we all come to take; I hope you know that you don't have to make it alone.

CHAPTER 1

Sometimes Courage Is the Heart of Love

Late winter sunlight streamed in on the quilt covering my legs. It was unusually intense and baked through the double layer of covers, causing my legs to sweat. I shifted uncomfortably, sat up, and wiped the sleep from my eyes. Suddenly, deep wracking sobs erupted from the center of my chest. I held a corner of the quilt over my face until the wave had passed. I wasn't even fully awake yet, and already I felt the huge weight of grief. It felt like a shroud, separating me, cutting me off from everything in my life: family, daily activities, our other cat, Acacia, the coming spring, my breath.

I'd been waking up like this for weeks. Each night when I went to sleep, I hoped for some small respite. Sometimes grief is so deep, so profound, that our subconscious cannot express it even in dreams. I prayed for nights like this. And I got them. No dreams. I was immensely grateful, but the trade-off was waking.

Most mornings, I would have gladly wiped dreams from my eyes; dreams would have ended there, replaced by the ordered sensibility of day. But waking had become like the beginning of a fully conscious bad dream that I had to endure, not in the privacy of my sleep state that would end with the coming of dawn, but in public. And sometimes, in places where sobbing and sorrow had to be borne discreetly.

I remembered the comment of an acquaintance of mine who found me sobbing in my car in a parking lot a few days previously.

"Get a grip," she had said. "He was only a cat."

The words reverberated through my head. Only a cat. Only a cat. Only a cat.

Cautiously, like a child pulling a scab from her knee, compelled by a mixture of pain and fascination, I began to recall the last three months of my life. The last three months of McTavish's life.

What made my grief almost unbearable was the added weight of guilt and self-blame. Remorse, heavier and more toxic, would come later. Having just received my bachelor's degree in alternative animal medicine, I was about to begin my graduate studies in veterinary homeopathy but was unsure if I was worthy to continue.

If anybody had been able to save McTavish, it should have been me. I should have known; I should have seen. Was I not paying attention? Later, I would come to understand that objectivity is a rare luxury when someone we love is ill. I would also come to understand that the self-blame I felt was more closely related to anger and a deep sense of powerlessness. It was easier, somehow, to accept all blame and responsibility myself, than to attempt a dialogue with others who had been involved in the last months of his life. My grief was too fresh, too raw, to attempt communication with anyone outside of my isolation.

Another scab, another memory, surfaced. Slowly, fascinated, I began to pick through the ruins and surprised myself with a small smile.

❦

I had gone to a landfill in the spring of 1983. A rural Maine landfill, where the poverty of the leavings glare at hurried visitors like silent accusations. I went to deposit several bags of garbage there, never dreaming I'd find anything of value to bring home. But I was approached by a newly mature, striped tabby cat who stood on hind legs and, placing his front paws on my knees, looked up expectantly into my face. I reached down and gathered him up into my arms; he offered no resistance.

For a dump cat, I thought he was in pretty good shape. I wondered about that for a long time. Was he such a good hunter that he was able to keep himself fed? Or had he wandered there from some neighboring house, out of boredom or simply because the hunting was good? I had heard grim rumors of the landfill attendants' attempts to keep the rat population at bay. Those poor creatures who managed to survive poisoning were simply used for target practice. I surmised that if this young cat was hunting in the dump, it was for the purpose of resolving his hunger, not his boredom. In the back of my mind, I recognized that he had a lot on the ball; he'd avoided poisoning and rats and if not bullets, then he had certainly overcome any fear of the roar from shotgun blasts.

He wasn't remarkable in any outward sort of way. I thought he was quiet and reserved and wonderfully well-mannered for a cat who had been forced to forage for every morsel. But it was his calmness and his general air of contentment that endeared him to me in the first place. That and the chummy way he would accompany me everywhere.

I'd always gotten to know my cats before naming them, and I had thought about naming him Chumley, because he was so chummy. But someone I once knew had a cat by the name of McTavish, and I thought it was a really great name for a cat, especially for a tabby cat, who resemble in their physical markings the Scottish Highland wild cats of the British Isles.

So, McTavish it was. And he liked it. You can always tell with cats when they like their names; they trill at you when you whisper it from another room, or if lying quietly beside you, they look up when you say it aloud. Soon there were numerous diminutive forms: Micky T, Tavish, Mr. T, and of course, Mc T.

Our adventures were numerous, spanning nearly a decade. We moved several times together. For six of those years, we lived with and learned to understand a ninety-seven-pound Doberman Pinscher, whose primary goal in life was to be a lapdog and who had an uncontrollable addiction to cat food. During one of our many moves, I was living in a temporary situation where I could not have animals. McTavish went to stay briefly at a friend's farm in the country. There, I hoped, he would wait until the next move when he could rejoin the family. Unfortunately, the farm was guarded by an older dog who barked incessantly, not so much for reasons of dominion or aggression, but more, I suspect, out of boredom. McTavish found the situation intolerable and left.

It took me three months to find him, but I never gave up. Even on those long and lonely nights when I would lie awake missing his presence on the bed, my intuition told me that, although he was in trouble, McTavish was still alive and he wanted to come home. The same intuition eventually led me to the two women who had taken him in and, in doing so, had saved his life. Our bond had grown strong and deep, in ways that miles or explanations could not weaken. It simply was. The memory of our reunion, so long delayed, is still crystal clear in my mind; how can I describe to you how delicious it is to be hugged by a cat?

He won my heart in a way that has forever changed my relationship with animals, and to him I owe a great debt. It was the intensity of our friendship that carried us through his last month of life, but it was also our bond that made his passing so deeply painful for me.

Up until the last three months of his life, McTavish had experienced no illnesses. He had, at one point, suffered from a series of debilitating seizures, caused by, I found out much too late, a neighbor who, fed up with his morning cat fights under her bedroom window, attempted resolution by flailing at both cats with a wooden broom handle. But illnesses, no. Not a single upper respiratory infection, not a sniffle, or a urinary tract episode. Nothing.

The local veterinarian who provided routine health care for my animal companions was well established in his practice. He had an affinity for horses, and in this rural area, he was in great demand. His manner reminded me of the quintessential country vet; he had a thoughtfulness and peacefulness about him unlike most humans I know. He was a nice fellow, soft-spoken, and gentle in his approach. Going to see him was like visiting with an uncle. Until that winter, all of our visits to him had been for routine health maintenance.

One day in early winter, I noticed that McTavish had a great deal of mouth odor. I also noticed that he was having trouble eating. Sometimes, he would approach his bowl, take a bite, and growl; other times, he would chew, but the food would fall out of his mouth and back into his bowl or onto the floor. I made an appointment for an examination.

During the first visit, two upper teeth were extracted. It seemed routine. When we returned home, I gave McTavish a dose of Arnica for the bruising caused by the extraction and some Phosphorus to help his body release the anesthesia. But subsequently, after the anesthesia wore off, he began to paw at his mouth and was still having difficulty chewing. Within a few days he was drooling copiously and seemed to have developed stomatitis, a nonspecific group of symptoms indicating inflammation of the mouth. Rationally and logically, I attributed the symptoms to abrasions in his mouth caused by the surgical procedure. I gave him Mercurius, a remedy commonly used for stomatitis. But his symptoms continued.

I made a second appointment for the vet to see him. McTavish was duly examined, and the vet concluded that McTavish's mouth was fine and no further treatment was necessary. I left the clinic feeling somewhat confused. I knew what I had been seeing but did not want to contradict this vet, with whom I'd had a working relationship for many years. We went home, McTavish drooling puddles on the towel lining his transport carrier, me filled with a panicky determination to find the remedy for his problem.

Over the next few days the stomatitis continued, and I began to puree McTavish's meals and feed him with a spoon. I bought jars of baby food and tubs of chicken liver, ruined a coffee-bean grinder, and bought a food blender. My kitchen had turned into a gourmet restaurant for felines.

At this point McTavish began to spend all of his time in the dark closet of an unused bedroom in the back of the house. This unnerved me more than his physical symptoms. He had always chummed up to me, sleeping on my bed at night. His isolating behavior left my hands cold and my heart thumping. I made a third appointment and brought McTavish to the vet for another examination.

Again, the vet insisted that nothing was wrong with his mouth. Gathering all my courage, I insisted that something was very wrong and that whatever needed to be done to properly diagnose the situation should be done quickly. I indicated that if McTavish needed to remain overnight and be anesthetized for examination that I was amenable to that possibility.

Before I left McTavish at the clinic, the vet told me that we needed to make sure that McTavish did not have cancer of the mouth. He would perform an examination to ascertain if this was the case, and he urged me to consider euthanasia if cancer was found because the outcome in such cases is usually very poor. I told him that I would make that decision if necessary because I really loved this cat and did not want to see him suffer.

The vet kept him overnight and removed a third tooth, this time a lower left molar. When I picked McTavish up the next day, the vet informed me that the molar tooth had abscessed and prescribed .75 grams of Amoxicillin to be given once a day for ten days. He offered one piece of positive news, "McTavish does not have cancer, which is a good thing."

With an unexpected flash of courage, I asked for a refund on my second office visit. After all, I insisted, I was told nothing was wrong and no further treatment was necessary. I paid for an office visit, I continued, swallowing almost audibly, and have had to bring him back a third time.

His face assumed an impassive stoniness as he ushered us out into the waiting room. He exchanged a few brief, private words with his receptionist behind the closed door of the examination room. She briskly swept past me on her way back to her desk and made an adjustment to my bill. In the parking lot, I walked slowly to my car, clutching the stamped bill in one hand and the lighter-than-ever transport carrier in the other. I felt very small and very heavy at the same time.

The stomatitis continued throughout the course of the antibiotic treatment. Within hours of the last dose, the left side of McTavish's face ballooned outward, and he became unable to swallow. He watched me with his one good eye from the dark recess of the closet. There was a finality, a resolution in that gaze. Panic rose like bile in my throat. I realized that we had a long way to go. A very long way. Things would never again be the same. And looking back, I realize that in that moment, my grieving process began.

I called a homeopathic veterinarian from southern New England, the same vet who had suggested the problem was stomatitis. At her recommendation I tried several homeopathic remedies, some with a small measure of success; the swelling was reduced, although McTavish still could not put anything other than liquids in his mouth without gagging.

This went on for another week, during which time I tried several other remedies suggested by the homeopathic vet. An abscess formed under McTavish's chin and drained but would not heal. I went back to the local vet's office and purchased a twenty-day supply of Clavamox to resolve the abscess. The abscess continued to fester, and the stomatitis continued unabated.

He still was spending all his time in the closet. I divided my time between making liquid meals for him, trying to get him to eat, and tracking down homeopathic remedies. It was at this time that I became aware of how emotionally exhausted I was. I was continuously on the brink of emotional overload, yet poised, waiting for the next development. Would he begin to get well, or would he continue to weaken, lose weight, and fade farther away? My heart and intuition picked mercilessly at the edge of my consciousness.

I plodded on with grim determination. We had been through much together, he and I, and we would get through this together also. We were bound by ties of love and fealty that nothing could break. I will not let go, I thought; I will not let you fall; we are bound together through time and all events; you are mine and I am yours.

A few days later, I called another veterinarian and asked for advice. We spent a few minutes discussing symptoms, possible diagnoses, and treatment options, but came to no conclusion other than the next step. I was told to bring McTavish to his clinic for examination the following morning.

That night I put my bed on the floor and arranged a portable foam mattress next to it, so he could sleep next to me. At the time, I didn't know why I did this, but I think McTavish did. I do remember waking in the quiet darkness of night, a tickle in the palm of my hand. McTavish had moved over as close to me as his discomfort would allow. His paw rested gently in the palm of my outstretched hand; he was flexing his toes, as though to squeeze my hand in quiet reassurance. It'll be OK, he seemed to say, our love is strong.

The next morning was difficult. I awoke with my breath stuck in my chest. Somewhere in the back of my mind, I knew the day was one I would remember for a long time to come. We made the trip in our usual fashion, he in his transport carrier in the front seat beside me, I driving with one arm slung companionably over the top of his carrier. He seemed unusually quiet as he lay on one of my sweatshirts, not even looking at me through the small opening in the side of the carrier. I drove very slowly, wanting those short twenty-three miles to last another lifetime. One more year, I thought. Please, just one more.

Upon examination, the vet found a hard swelling in the lower jaw below the site of extraction. He suggested two possibilities. The first was easier to resolve. If it was an abscess below the gum line in the jawbone, that could be dealt with surgically and followed up with heavy doses of antibiotics. The other possibility was more sinister: a malignant growth. I was instructed to leave him there for a surgical examination. The vet would X-ray his jaw, clean the site of previous extraction, determine the extent of the abscess, and, if necessary, perform a bone biopsy. I should call around noon, when the clinic would have a definite diagnosis to report.

I spent the morning in the company of a good friend. We sat in her home, filling in the hours until I could call with the distraction of talking about her work as a potter. Time stretched, lagged, faltered, and seemed to stall. Finally noon came, but dialing the phone number of the clinic felt dreadful. It was a call I knew I didn't want to make. I suddenly had an intimate acquaintance with the phrase "hoping against all hope."

The vet was decisive in his assessment. X-ray and surgical examination revealed a malignant growth on the lower jaw, below the site of previous extractions. The growth was large; it had misplaced the jawbone, severing it in half. The tumor had pushed against the teeth above it, exposing their tender roots and causing them to abscess. That's why they needed to be removed. But he gave no explanation about why the previous vet had removed several teeth on McTavish's upper jaw. About that, he simply didn't comment.

His voice continued to buzz at me through the telephone line. During the surgical examination he had removed as much of the growth as possible. He had also taken a biopsy for histopathologic diagnosis, which would be sent to a university lab in southern New England.

As though from a great distance, I heard him recommend that I have McTavish put to sleep because he had lost much weight in the last weeks and the removal of malignant growth and surrounding bone would make it impossible for him to eat. He also said that the malignancy had spread to such a degree that it would continue to worsen. He was unsure if McTavish could withstand another round of surgery, even if more of the growth could be removed.

The phone call began to take on a nightmarish edge. I suddenly could not remember all the questions I had planned to ask. Perhaps they were moot points at this juncture. As if anticipating my reaction, the vet informed me that McTavish was still under the effects of the anesthesia. He was comfortable, in no pain, he said, and would not begin to regain consciousness for several more hours. He suggested that I come by the clinic around four that afternoon. I could spend the interval giving some thought to what decision I would want to make.

I fled home. Not for comfort, because all the elements of our life together would be spread out painfully before me, a mute, savage testimony of my failure. I fled for privacy. I needed privacy to think and reflect. To cry, possibly, at least to let my emotions loose on my face.

I had been holding my face painfully immobile for many weeks. I had plenty of reasons. I somehow thought that if McTavish could see the fear etched there, he would lose hope. His hope, his grasp on living, was my only rope; without it he would slide so far downward that I would not be able to bring him back. Also, I had many other responsibilities; if my emotions were allowed to surface, I was afraid that a huge dam would break, a flood that I could not control. And I had to maintain some control over something; my emotions seemed the only thing left to me to govern.

In the kitchen, the blender stared accusingly at me: you failed! it screamed silently. I swept past it toward the bathroom, to wash my face and brush my teeth, hoping for a moment of refreshment, the chance to catch my breath. There was a brassy, burned taste in my mouth that was suddenly revolting.

I wandered throughout the house, listlessly and without any real purpose. There were the food bowls from last night, washed and neatly stacked on the kitchen counter. They too accused me: he had had to skip breakfast because of the possibility of anesthesia, he was already faint and weak with hunger, yet on top of all his pain, you denied him even breakfast. I avoided looking at the blender; there was more to its sharpness than its blades.

In the back bedroom, I found I could touch nothing. His smell was there, that delicious smell of cat fur, but underneath it lurked the odor of an illness gone awry. I looked at the clumps of fur stuck to his pillow, clumps that he had pulled off more recently, ragged bits of him that I had somehow missed in my cleaning. That I had missed them was possibly from denial, but more likely it had happened as the result of the tunnel vision I had come to exercise, as more and more of him—and only him—filled the entire scope of my visual field. I wanted to touch these remnants of him, to rub their silkiness between my fingers, to drink in the smell of him. But I could not. Instead, I left the room, shutting the door quietly behind me and went to wait on the back stoop for the school bus.

Inevitably, the time had come to be back at the veterinary clinic. My son and I arrived on time, and after a brief wait in the reception area, we were led into an adjoining examination room. There the vet explained to me that McTavish was just waking from the anesthesia. He would not be fully conscious, but he would know me, and he would be able to hear me and feel my touch. What had I decided, he wanted to know. I could not bring myself to say the words "euthanasia" or "put to sleep"; but the vet nodded solemnly at my utterance to "not let him suffer."

Momentarily, he was in my arms, weakly looking up at me.

He trilled a greeting: Hello! It is you. You are finally here, and I am so glad to see you. He could hardly hold his head up. Helping him, I was immeasurably grateful for the miracle of anesthetic. I tried to ease him over, to get a look at the ravage of his face. It was an exercise in pointlessness. There was nothing to see. The tumor and surrounding tissue had been removed, leaving a depression in his face that was covered with clean-shaven skin and a small, neat row of several stitches.

We held a lifetime in that moment, looking into one another's eyes. All our days together had come to this one point in time. He was still strong; I could see it in his eyes. He was very much present in his physical body, and our bond was still vibrant and alive. I could see time stretching beyond us, him with the remnants of a face, me trying to feed him, both of us faltering, determined to postpone the inevitable. It could not be. Sometimes love must submit to courage. Sometimes courage must be the heart of love. I kissed him on the good side of his face, in that place that I had kissed him thousands of times before; I love you, I said simply. I nodded to the vet, who gave McTavish a small injection in his thigh; he wilted in my arms, and I placed him on the table before me, knowing that the longest moment was yet to come.

Had I known how the vet was going to administer the euthanasia medication, I would have stopped him and requested a less traumatic method. But I did not know. I had attended other euthanasia procedures with many other cats; the vein in the forearm is tied off, the larger-than-life dose of barbiturate injected; peace softens the ragged edges of pain that line the face and finally steals across the remaining flicker of awareness that still shines out of yellow or green cat eyes. The spirit escapes the tired body through the pupils, now open wide. I had no premonition, no clue that this was to be a very different ending.

Holding my breath and not wanting to see the hypodermic, I shut my eyes firmly. I opened them just in time to see a very long needle being plunged into the center of his chest. McTavish cried out, one wail that was suddenly silenced as his heart stopped. The sound reverberated in the room, in my ears, in my head, coming heavily to rest in the center of my chest. In a blur of tears, I reached for him and grasped him to my breast. I felt as though I had failed.

❦

Four years have passed. Much has happened in that time. The lab report came back and confirmed the diagnosis of malignancy. I did finish school, receiving my master's degree. It was a hard sell, forcing myself to make the choice to return and finish, but I have learned that it is more difficult and emotionally painful not to follow my heart and passion. Being in school provided me with two more years to heal before returning to the world of humans and helping them achieve their successes or holding their hands while they made difficult decisions.

But McTavish seemed to remain with me for several months after his death. During those weeks, I did think at times that I could hear him walking through the house. He had a peculiar gate; an injury he had sustained left one hip slightly off-kilter, and he could no longer fully retract his claws on that foot. When he walked, it was with a faint clicking sound of claws on hardwood floors.

Several times I thought I saw him walk into a room. A faint shadowy form would glide in front of my chair, or appear in the lower edge of my peripheral vision, a shape that carried within it the particular pattern of his tabby stripes. At these appearances, I would strain my eyes to see more clearly, but in refocusing, the outline would fade, and what I thought I had seen would be suddenly gone.

He appeared in my dreams on more than one occasion. Among the many people I have talked with about the death of their animal companions, this seems to be a common experience. In these dreams my other cat, Acacia, would always be there with us. Night after night, I would try to pick him up to take him home with us, but my fingers would slip through his transparent form, and he would fade away into nothingness. At the end of each of these dreams, I was able to pick up Acacia, and we would walk away down a footpath, to return home without him. Even in my dream state, I was healing, as I reconciled myself to the fact that McTavish was in a different place than our world. He was everywhere; we were here.

I did love Acacia throughout my grieving process, but for several days I could not bear for her to be anywhere near me. Having her sit in my lap was unthinkable, intolerable. I am sure that her grief was very deep; not only had she lost her friend, the big guy she loved to the point of worship, but she also had to endure her grief alone because my grief totally isolated me from other parts of my life—even her. I regret not being emotionally available to her during those days, but we have now bonded in our own special way, and as the animals in our lives do, I think she has forgiven me for my frailty.

We have even found room in our lives to accept another cat, a sweet female named Cat, who came from a disturbing situation. She was a cat no one wanted and had her own grief and trauma to contend with because (we suspect) she witnessed the suicide of her first human companion.

From both my cats, I have learned much about how animals grieve and how they heal slowly, much like humans. Together, in our different ways and for different reasons, we have all experienced a process of healing. Survivors of grief, we understand and comfort one another and tenderly let our bonds deepen over time. We know that these bonds will be tried and tested, but we also know that our courage to love one another will withstand anything that destiny has in store for us.

I invite you, in the pages ahead, to travel with me as I recount my journeys with several animal companions. Perhaps the path that you have traveled parallels mine. Perhaps our paths have been somewhat divergent, but we have seen some of the same landmarks along the way.

What these trusting and loving individuals taught me and how I grew from their compassionate and timeless lessons has changed me for all time. During this process, I sought out the writings of others in an attempt to articulate the physical and emotional experiences I had on this voyage. Some of the authors wrote from a scientific perspective; others simply mirrored my own experiences without offering tangible scientific proof. I came to believe that while singular events constitute unexplained phenomena, events that occur many times over are something more than mere happenstance. Perhaps it is true that the voice of the heart speaks in a language that has no known words.

CHAPTER 2

Bruno

I had gone to town to shop on a Friday afternoon. As I arrived in the supermarket parking lot, I saw a small poodle running around—very frightened and very wet. He was dashing to and fro, back and forth, nearly out of his wits. I managed to catch him before the wheels of a car entering or leaving the parking lot did, and I checked his collar for tags. Finding none, I phoned the police station from a public phone in the entryway of the store and asked an officer to come and see about a loose dog.

Bruno was shivering and wet from dashing through late winter puddles in the parking lot. His underbelly and legs were matted with small balls of ice, and he trembled with terror. I removed my down vest, bundled him in it, and set him on the top of the only surface off the floor—a trash can inside the entryway. He was such a small, trembling armful! While I waited for the officer to arrive, a boy of about fifteen showed up with a German shepherd in tow. He said his name was Johnny and that the dog had belonged to him last summer before he gave it to his next-door neighbor. Johnny said that the woman no longer wanted the dog and that morning

19

had asked another teenage boy in the neighborhood to come and get it and "dump it somewhere in town."

He had seen Bruno in the parking lot a short time before and had placed him in a shopping cart while he went home to ask his mother if he could bring him home. Of course, Bruno escaped from the cart while Johnny was gone and had worked himself into a pretty good lather before I arrived on the scene.

I could tell that this little dog needed immediate attention—Rescue Remedy or Aconite for panic and terror, removal of the ice, hot water bottles and blankets for the beginning stages of hypothermia. While a shelter would see to his needs, there was likely to be at least an hour's delay, and I was determined to see that he was cared for immediately.

I was concerned that his emotional distress would have long-lasting effects if not treated with homeopathic remedies. I also realized that above everything else, Bruno needed to be in a place that was very quiet and calm. This would make all the difference in the world, allowing him to recover both mentally and physically from his ordeal. A ride in a police car to a noisy shelter of barking dogs and a cold concrete floor lined only with an old blanket for bedding would only have negative results.

Within a few minutes the officer arrived on the scene. I talked the officer into letting me have the dog, and then the officer talked Johnny into letting me have the dog. The officer left after making some notes in his notebook, and Johnny and I stood looking at one another. He looked at me, he looked at Bruno. And tears welled up in his eyes. Bruno shivered, and I quickly wrote down my phone number and gave it to Johnny. Bruno and I went home.

There must have been an angel nearby when I bought my car, and he or she made sure that it had a great heater in it, one that would be used in emergencies just like this. With hot air blasting out of all the heater ducts, we wound our way slowly home. This little guy could not believe his luck. Warmth, a car to ride in, the front seat—and my very own down vest to boot! What looked like a smile appeared on Bruno's face, and I knew I was doing the right thing.

At home a few minutes later, my cat, Acacia, took one look at Bruno and went into the living room and threw up on the floor. "You've gone over the top, now, Mom," she seemed to be saying. Then without so much as a backward glance, her tail followed her under a chair. Injured cat pride would be almost palpable in our house for the next few days, but for a cat like Acacia, such emotional temper tantrums are part of life. As often as we can, we bend and temper our lives and lifestyle to suit her and soothe her, but sometimes other animals come into our lives with immediate needs. And in the end, she usually forgives our betrayal, if only because the strays who find their way to us turn out to be temporary visitors.

Bruno settled in for a while. Out came the Aconite and blankets while Acacia found high ground from which to observe the most heinous of crimes in the world of a cat—lavishing loving attention on a dog (good grief!). Bruno, bundled to the ears, listened to the furnace roar and watched me cook his lunch.

Within a few minutes, a big bowl of steaming scrambled eggs and tofu with chunks of wheat bread floating in a sea of rich, warm beef gravy was placed in front of him. He needed no coaxing; wiggling out of the blankets, he dashed for the bowl. When it was finished, dessert was a long drink of well water. A nap was in order after this difficult ordeal, and once again, cozy blankets were a welcome haven.

The afternoon wore quietly on. Either the heat of the house or the weight of the blankets woke Bruno, but once awake he realized that it was time for doing a "dog chore." During my search for a piece of rope to serve as a leash, the chore was finished on the kitchen floor. Little did I know that I was soon to be trained to meet the varying needs of a wonderful little dog. A call to the police officer I had met earlier that day revealed the name of the previous owner and a bit more of Bruno's history. He had lived with Joline, an alcoholic, who thought it would be neat to name her dog after her favorite bar. Bruno had spent much of his time outdoors, waiting. His whole life was one of waiting—for food, for warmth, for attention. And unfortunately, the kind of attention that Bruno had experienced was anything but kind. As far as I could tell, he had never had a bath (and he was almost a year old), and his ears had never been cleaned. A few phone calls later, I ascertained that none of the vets had any records of basic medical care; he'd not been wormed nor had a rabies vaccination.

Picking up my son, Forrest, after his French lessons at school posed a problem. Exposure to more cold wind might not be very good for Bruno, but being abandoned again by being left alone in the house would be much worse emotionally. I was also a responsible cat mother and instinctively knew that Acacia would not want me to leave her at home with a strange dog. So another ride in the car was in order. And Bruno, proudly wearing his new down vest, happily claimed, in the name of Poodledom, the newly found backseat territory for his own.

Forrest's initial reaction to seeing Bruno was a snicker. "*That's* a dog?" Bruno, suddenly very protective, indicated with a babyish growl that I belonged exclusively to him. The bond, I realized, was beginning to form, and for what it was worth, for good or for bad, Bruno and I were on the brink of creating our history together.

It was the arrival home, back to my house, that resolved the anguish for Bruno. Incredulously, he came back to the place where food and warmth had been experienced with such relief earlier that day. He didn't seem to mind when I left him at home with Forrest while I went back to town to retrieve the forgotten groceries and the new items I'd added to my list: dog food and chew toys.

A late winter storm arrived in the small hours of Saturday morning. Winds buffeted the house, sleet pelted the windows, and going outdoors for dog chores was an event in itself. Still the kitchen was warm, food came regularly, and kindness was a healing medicine. During the next few days, while he settled comfortably into routine and consistency, Bruno began to accumulate his own possessions. Leash, food and water bowls, a travel kennel that served as his very own nighttime bed, rawhide chews, a favorite corner in the kitchen lined with a fluffy sleeping bag where two baseboard heaters abutted in a corner, and of course, a special place directly in the middle of the walkway for depositing his dog chores.

The accumulation of road salt, dirt, and old feces that hung in clumps to the fur on his back legs made a bath a necessity. Bruno sat very still in the bathtub and luxuriated in the warm, sudsy water. Every so often he would look up at my eyes to ask if everything was all right, not quite daring to believe that human hands could be so gentle and slow, that warmth could be so delicious and relaxing. When I wrapped him in big towels to dry, he hiccuped and sighed several times; it was an emotional moment for both of us. After a modest combing and an extensive massage, Bruno fell into a deep, sound sleep.

We are not a dog-oriented family, a statement of fact that Acacia will readily agree with. Poodles require expensive clippings due to the way their hair grows, not to mention a bath almost every other day. And Bruno was a dirt magnet, picking up every tiny piece of lint and dirt he came across. The wonderful smell of his bath and the luster of his clean coat wore off in less than a day, and by Sunday his face was sticky with food and his feet were filthy.

Not only was I unable to accommodate adding dog baths to my daily roster of tasks, but I also had a job to go to, and leaving Bruno at home every day was not a workable solution. Cats enjoy long hours of solitude, basking in the supremacy of total control of an empty house; dogs do not. Dogs, being the social animals they are, like to go everywhere, which is fine, but I could not take him to work with me. I began to spread the word that this great little guy was screening potential families.

By Monday the calls were coming in; little dogs like Bruno are frequently in high demand. Appointments were made for several families to come later in the week and meet Bruno, so that he could choose his new owners. I pictured Bruno living in doggy heaven with an older couple who perhaps lived in a trailer. The woman would make afghans that would be draped all over the couch and bed, and there would be one or two in the car; the man would look forward to taking Bruno for a drive every Wednesday night to get the latest edition of the weekly paper. Bruno and his family would watch the evening news together every night from the cozy comfort of the afghan-padded living-room couch. They would be retired and devote their time to Bruno's comfort and be his constant companions. Weekly appointments would be kept at the dog groomer's, but Bruno would not be subjected to pink nail polish and hair ribbons; his would be a pampered, yet dignified life. He would get to eat real food, not from cans, and he would have his very own box of squeaky toys to entice his favorite humans into friendly games of fetch and toss. In short, he would be loved almost to the bursting point, almost more than his little heart could endure. The center of attention, Bruno would never want for anything again; his would be a world of fullness to finally make up for all the lack of things he never got.

Tuesday I had an appointment in a large city to the south, a two-hour drive. After speaking with my friend Linda about the pros and cons of taking Bruno with me or leaving him alone for six and a half hours, I decided to take him with me for the day. It was a new experience for both of us. My friend Bill offered to drive, leaving me free to devote all my attention to making Bruno feel safe and comfortable. Into the backseat went his sleeping bag, chew toys, leash, and food and water bowls. We were off on a grand adventure, most of which Bruno spent either sleeping in my lap in the front seat or commandeering the observation deck of the rear window.

On the harbor, the bustling city was cold; the wet March wind howled down the main throughway. The only place to park the car was in a freezing parking garage, and Bruno was relieved when he realized that he would spend the entire day no more than a foot away from me. I carried him around wrapped in the bulk of my heavy down coat when we were not taking "walkies" for dog chores or actually attending to my appointment. He never left my side, never complained. It was a day of learning to trust all over again, seeing for the first time that he could go somewhere and not be abandoned, that there was consistency in life, that he need not be afraid. Someone loved him and wouldn't leave him. He trembled at each new experience. The most awful one was going with me into the woman's restroom, but we managed, and he got a drink of water. Lunch was shared in the car on the way home, and puppy pit stops were frequent.

The coup de grace was arriving home again. He barked joyfully as we pulled into the familiar driveway, grabbed his chew toy, and got ready to visit his very own yellow spot in the middle of the walkway. Bruno fairly danced as we came into the kitchen, and Acacia fled to the other end of the house.

We had been working—both of us—on the business of getting housebroken. It was not clear to me if Bruno had ever been housebroken. I was uncertain if he had just been put outside for long periods of time and spanked frequently for voiding indoors, or if he knew about going outdoors but was having a difficult time due to unfamiliar surroundings and his recent trauma. My friend Dan in Vermont, who counseled me about such matters, explained to me "the rules." It soon became clear to me that I needed to be trained to communicate clearly and swiftly and, of course, consistently. I never had to use the can of pennies to interrupt an accident in the kitchen. I never even had to raise my voice to Bruno; a soft, gentle "no" was sufficient, followed by a quick and gentle exit outdoors. After a few maneuvers our rhythm was established, and "do you want to go out?" would elicit the proper response; once outside, a "hurry up" would get things started, and praises of "good boy!" would light up Bruno's eyes and bring what looked like a smile to his face. As astounding as it seems, we were both trained within a day, except for a few accidents, which were my fault for not being attentive enough.

Tuesday night Bruno got the shivers and began to sneeze. His big city adventure had stressed his recovering immune system. I set about figuring out his constitutional remedy; a dose of this when he was exhibiting acute symptoms of his chronic state would soon put him to rights.

Pulsatilla was Bruno's constitutional remedy. He fits the psychological profile of shyness that is almost torture, the wistful wanting of what is offered, and the subsequent dashing to the ankles or lap of the human he wants to trust, and burying his face in a gesture of submission. His, too, is the trusting heart that has been broken, yet he wants with every fiber of his being to dare to trust again, for that is the only way he will ever find safety and security. Wanting to be held and having his symptoms relieved by this action, sneezing, wet eyes, and symptoms brought on by exposure to cold wet winds were other symptoms that Bruno had, all of which came under the sphere of Pulsatilla.

I knew that he would be going to a new home soon. It was important for him to learn trust from me, to get his emotional symptoms resolved quickly, but not to bond too tightly, because when he left here for a new and permanent home, too close a bond would hurt, and he would experience a feeling of abandonment all over again. Because of this, there would not be enough time to use ascending potencies; his symptoms were acute suddenly and would respond with only mild aggravation to a 30x dose, so that is what I gave him. A healing sleep came gently as the Pulsatilla went to work. In an hour he woke up and was like a new dog. Gone were the shivers, sneezing, and wet eyes; he stalked the kitchen (and Acacia) with a new confident resolve.

Wednesday brought Allison to meet Bruno. He did not like her very much. She wore big, heavy riding boots that frightened him badly. It occurred to both of us that Bruno might have experienced boots like those before and not necessarily in a pleasant way. Trembling with fear, he hesitantly accepted proffered treats of tiny pieces of meat from her hand but cautiously avoided the boots. Allison explained that their family dog, a small terrier mix, had been stolen from the family car last summer. Missing their terrier, they wanted another small dog and would give Bruno a good home. He would only be alone from eight o'clock in the morning until two in the afternoon, she said. My spirits fell, and Bruno asked to get into my lap. She took his picture twice at the end of their visit, one to take home to show her family and one that she gave to me. Bruno was relieved when Allison left and sat on my feet for a long while.

An hour later Beth and Robert came to meet Bruno. His response was trembling fear again. We all sat closely in chairs in the middle of the sunny kitchen, Bruno on my lap, refusing to get down.

To his amazement (and to mine), Beth and Robert both took doggie biscuits out of their pockets and offered them to Bruno. He licked the one that Robert held out but pulled back when Robert reached out to pat him. In a few moments Bruno leaned over and gave Beth a lick on the face. Beth looked over at her husband and said with her eyes, Robert, I must have this dog.

I placed Bruno gently in Robert's eager arms. He tried to explain. Two weeks ago their poodle had been hit by a car and had died instantly. Robert's eyes began to fill with tears as he told the story, his voice wavered slightly, and Beth, seeing his difficulty, took up the tale.

It was hard, she said, having the box of squeaky toys in the living room, untouched all this time. The afghan she'd made for Bowser lay washed and unused at the foot of their bed where he used to sleep at night.

Suddenly, she looked straight into my eyes and said in a desperate soft voice, "We'll take him right now, if you'll let us have him. We'll give him so much love, he won't ever want for anything. We have no children, and our cat really misses Bowser—almost as much as we do. We have everything he will ever need, a whole box of toys, a travel carrier for very long rides." Her voice picked up pace, and the words came out in a breathy rush. "We'll never leave him alone for even a minute; he will go everywhere with us, in the car with me, and in the truck with Robert to get the paper in the evening. We'll never let him out of our sight, he won't even go outside by himself."

I asked, incredulously, "Right now? Without even a second thought? Right this minute? You want him right now?" My maternal instincts were kicking in, and I realized with a tinge of panic that this was it. Although we had bonded, I didn't have the lifestyle and means to give Bruno everything he deserved; this was his big chance to have everything he had always wanted. Did I love him enough to let him go?

I looked over at Beth who was holding out photographs. The interior of their trailer home was awash with vividly colored afghans draped over the couch, on chairs, everywhere.

"And this is a picture of Bowser." She held out another snapshot. Bowser lay on their bed in canine bliss, his head resting on pillows, covered to just below the ears in a bright green-and-cream afghan—sound asleep.

Bruno heaved a deep sigh. He was snuggled down into Robert's lap; both had a look of deep contentment and bliss on their faces. Beth and Robert looked at each other, exchanged smiles, looked longingly at Bruno, and expectantly at me.

My stomach heaved and my heart felt painful and heavy. "Yes," I said, "we've been waiting for you." Angels danced in heaven as I gathered leash, food bowl, bedding, toys, and cans of dog food.

It was suddenly difficult to see, and things looked very blurry. Hearing his worldly goods being moved around, Bruno sat up in Robert's lap, anxiously looking at me. It was not going to be easy for him, I realized, but waiting longer after bonding more closely would be even more difficult.

Robert stood with Bruno in his arms. "Let's go home, Mother," he said to his wife, as he gazed at Bruno.

Bruno let himself be carried out the door. There was no struggle, no whimper. Much to Bruno's delight, Beth and Robert had a car just like mine. His sleeping bag went into the backseat, next to the afghan lining the rear observation deck. With Bruno's belongings in the trunk, Robert and Bruno climbed into the front passenger seat, as Beth took the steering wheel.

I leaned over and gave Bruno a big hug and kiss. "I love you," I said, "enough to let you go." Robert never looked up at me; he kept his eyes on the little black dog clasped firmly in his arms.

"This," he said, gesturing at the bright green afghan he and Bruno were sitting on, "is the car blanket for the dog."

"You can cry now," said Beth.

"I will, but I think I'll wait till I get into the house," I said, smiling. And they were gone.

The wind whipped around the house, foretelling another storm on the way. There was no leash tied to the railing of the kitchen stoop. The yard seemed desolate and empty. I looked at the trees thrashing back and forth in the steel-gray sky. Love is sometimes most difficult and painful, I thought.

But within the loss and grief there was a profound sense of joy and gratitude—and awe. This, I realized, is a moment of living in grace. How tender and full is the experience of life, how fragile, how fleeting.

Later in the evening I called. "How is Bruno settling in?" I asked. He was having the time of his life. He had already commandeered the box of squeaky toys in the living room, the observation deck in the car, and the front seat of Robert's truck on a jaunt to get the evening paper. After a huge supper Bruno took over the middle of the living-room couch, with his head resting in Robert's lap, and everyone watched the evening news together.

While I was talking to Beth on the phone, Bruno went over and wet his toybox (It's mine, he seemed to be saying, and I am marking it). Robert interrupted the accident with a soft "no" and took him outside immediately. Not wishing to further impose on quality family time, I said good-bye with the reminder that I would be over to see Bruno in a week or so, not so soon as to confuse him but to say hello and let him know that I am happy for him.

How could I have known that the ideal family would show up for Bruno? How could I have known that life in a trailer filled with afghans, squeaky toys, and so much love was waiting for him? My only explanation is angels; sometimes doing the right thing gives rewards beyond measure.

So my heart was both heavy and light, sad and happy. I had wanted so very much to enfold this wonderful young dog into my arms and give him everything good that a dog deserves. How could I trust that he would have adventures beyond imagination or that he would never want for anything ever again? It was simply hard to believe that I had done everything for him that he needed me to do, hard to believe that there would not come a time when my intervention would be needed again. It was not that I lacked faith in Beth and Robert. Every fiber of my being and Bruno's reaction to them assured me that they were the perfect people for him. The fact was that since I met him, many things in his life had been getting better and better. Still, I could not get over the nagging feeling that I, like so many people before me, had abandoned him.

That night, as I lay in bed waiting for sleep, Acacia arrived with the answer. The faint perfume of shampoo drifted into my room from the bath across the hall, the very shampoo that Bruno had been bathed with the day before. Its smell reminded me of him and aroused my sense of loss. Acacia came stealthily into my room and jumped on the bed. Soon she nuzzled my hand with her nose, a delicate purr rumbling in her throat, a reminder of our bond of trust and friendship. I had always done my best by and for her, she seemed to tell me.

And I had done my best for Bruno, too. My own rules and standards about such things are very high indeed. I had passed my own test, about that I had no doubt. I realized that my heart would heal, as did Bruno's. I had loved him enough to let him go.

CHAPTER 3

Human-Animal Bonds

Konrad Lorenz was known as a naturalist, an animal ethnologist, and a biologist. In his most famous animal behavior study, he raised a flock of goslings and discovered that if young geese were taken from their mother at a critical period in their development, they would imprint on (or identify with) any being that supplied them with nourishment, shelter, and companionship.[1] Lorenz found that some of the goslings he raised so thoroughly imprinted on their surrogate human mothers that they preferred humans to other geese.

Imprinting takes place with the young of other species as well. Puppies are a good case in point. Someone seeking a companion dog and wanting to establish a solid rapport with him or her will frequently obtain a puppy between the ages of four and fourteen weeks. In this way, through imprinting at an early age, the puppy will establish a closer bond with the human than with other dogs.

Lorenz also believed that dogs especially, owing to their high intelligence, were capable of lying or at least of distorting the truth to serve their own ends.[2] They do this, he asserted, to cover up embarrassment (for example, from mistakenly barking at their human companions), to gain attention and sympathy, or to elicit a desired rsponse from gullible humans. He frequently asserted that dogs are physically sensitive but that they love to be pitied and are quick to learn how to arouse the sympathy of tenderhearted humans.

Lorenz had a remarkable relationship with one of his own dogs, Stasi. This dog, he claimed, was very capable of distorting the truth to get a desired response from him.[3] On a bicycling tour, after a minor injury to her left forepaw, Stasi would become instantly lame if the direction they were taking was not to her liking. However, upon taking a route that she did like, the feigned lameness would suddenly disappear, only to reappear again should an unpleasant task (such as guarding his bicycle for long periods of time) be asked of her. Such intricate relationships between dogs and their human companions take years to evolve, with participants learning behavioral cues from one another over long periods of time. Through trial and error, the companions work through the process of gaining mutual trust based on love and respect.

The "working" dogs of the Delta Society in Renton, Washington, are intentionally raised to have close bonds with humans. The Delta Society provides a network for humans with animal companions, including volunteers, health care providers, psychologists, and scientists who believe in the therapeutic and beneficial relationships between animals and humans. One of their programs is the Pet Partners Program, in which human–animal teams are licensed to spend time with people in nursing homes, hospitals, prisons, schools, and other treatment facilities.[4] Pet Partners human–animal teams provide therapy and friendship for people who would otherwise not come in contact with animals.

Many animal behaviorists and veterinarians assert that relationships between animals and humans are interdependent, both emotionally and mentally.[5] Animal companions are like human children, dependent on their caregivers for food, shelter, protection, guidance, affection, and companionship. Animals identify with their human companions, much like an animal with its mother, for a sense of security. The relationship that evolves from such an interaction helps animals to find their place in the social order of the larger group of individuals whose existence is in relationship to one another.

Relationships between animals and humans may become so intricate that they may learn to communicate on intangible levels. J. Allen Boone, author of *Kinship With All Life,* specialized in human–animal communication and believed that animals often behave in ways that humans expect them to behave, by picking up behavioral and attitudinal clues from their human companions.[6] Boone also believed that animals are aware of other intangible clues from their human companions, such as telepathically reading their thoughts and sensing fear. He exemplifies this theory in his accounts of a dog, Strongheart, and a pet fly, called Freddie. Strongheart was a German shepherd who appeared in movies in the 1950s, and Boone met him when he was hired to care for Strongheart while his trainer was away on a business trip. Strongheart could, it seems, detect people who were dishonest and anticipated Boone's thoughts and plans. Freddie, the fly, demonstrated similar telepathic receptivity; he would come when telepathically called and behave as requested through telepathic communication with Boone.

Environmental factors such as changes in an animal's environment, home life, or daily activities may also influence the behavior of animals. Many animals exhibit jealousy when a new baby or a new animal companion is brought into the family group. Such emotions stem from a deep fear that their very security is at stake. Restructuring in the social order of the family (or pack or pride hierarchy), consistency of the food supply or attention, even territory boundaries may lie at the root of an animal's behavior change.

The stress of moving to a new house, schedule changes, or the illness of his or her primary human companion can also induce behavioral changes in an animal. These stressors result in feelings of insecurity on the part of the animal, who sees his or her very survival as dependent on the actions and activities of the human with whom he or she has bonded.

Loss of attention and real or imagined threats to security may manifest as a variety of observable symptoms: vomiting; diarrhea; excessive licking, chewing, and scratching of body parts; and voiding the bladder or bowels in unacceptable places. Such manifestations of physical and emotional "illnesses" are an animal's attempt to elicit attention, and any attention, no matter how negative, is better than no attention at all. This is particularly true of obese animals who overeat as the result of only having interactions with their owners during mealtimes.

While all animals seek attention and relationships with their human companions, there are basic social differences between dogs and cats. Dogs view their human companions as members of the pack, and all pack members have a special place in the order of the group. The hierarchy of a canine pack is the backbone of its survival: each member and form of communication has a specific and vital function within the group.[7] Most dogs view their masters as the alpha (or leader) dog in the pack, and are as submissive to this alpha human as they would be to an alpha dog within a similar social grouping. Generally, dogs who are subordinate to their human companions make the best animal companions (from the human point of view). The dog is the one animal who has so radically altered its whole way of living, and its entire sphere of interests, that it has become domestic in a very true sense.[8] The appeal of a relationship with a dog is that it is a bond of true friendship, a unique spiritual partnership.

The feline, however, remains truly wild within the framework of the pack structure (called a pride), despite what is seen by humans as becoming housebroken. Many cat owners will humorously attest that their humble homes are graced by cats who, if not for such fine accommodations and tasty fare, would seek other lodgings. Most humans think that it is this flagrant uncompromising independence on the part of the cat, coupled with its astounding return after each hunting foray, that makes the creature so endearing. It is a popular belief that one may never own a cat but is instead owned by the cat and only for the convenience of the cat.

However, the traditional human concept of the nature of the cat is now changing as astounding new observations of cats' lives have come to light in *The Tribe of Tiger*. In this eloquent book, author Elizabeth Marshall Thomas reveals the complexity and sophistication of the cat pride, an intricate mesh of behaviors and codes that rival the social order of the canine pack. What once was thought of as a fierce and survival-oriented grouping, Thomas has illuminated as a finely woven and highly evolved system of elaborate interactions. Not all interaction within a cat pride is oriented toward survival; important aspects also include trust, nurture, and felicity.[9]

It is important that we not be remiss in dismissing the special relationship between cats and their human companions. Once bonded emotionally with a cat, many humans remark that they are irrevocably changed in ways they could not have previously imagined. As with interactions with their own kind, cats seem to instill in humans deep ties of unbreakable fealty, ties that often last well beyond the phenomenon we call death. To be claimed by a cat, indeed to be owned by a cat, is to pass some unpassable test. Once we have earned this sacred stature, there are few irreversible mistakes we can make; like being knighted, being claimed by a cat is an honor that can never be forfeited.

Those who live with animals, whether dog or cat or another species, will insist that their relationships with their particular animal friends are special beyond comparison. In our relationships with the animals in our lives, there are times when certain crises arise. They become jealous of a new family member; they become emotionally needy; they exhibit "outrageous" behaviors; they experience illness; and they remind us of our own mortality as they experience their own death process.

We can all understand what our animal companions want and need if we simply take the time to listen to them. Such attempts on our part to understand their language is best done by being friends with them. In the process, we develop significant relationships and lasting bonds, often of such strength and endurance that our meager human offerings pale in comparison. When we truly come to love the animals in our care, we need no explanation to understand that the heart that is loved never forgets.

Seemingly ordinary provisions for your animal may ease the impact of life transitions or crises on everyone involved. Attending to their diets; making sure they get enough exercise, playtime, and sunlight; providing their own beds; correcting misbehavior in a loving way; and caring for the animal who is ill or in the death process seem simple enough considerations. Yet, these basic activities not only engage us in their health and life processes but also deepen the bond of friendship. Below are some common questions that you might like to explore to gauge the bond between you and your animal companion.

DIET

- Do I feed my animal friend a wide variety of natural foods?
- Do I feed my animal friend canned food because it is convenient for me, or do I feed him or her what he or she likes?

- Do I separate mealtime and playtime, or do I only pay attention to my animal friend during mealtime?

EXERCISE AND PLAYTIME

- Do I schedule regular playtimes with my animal friend?
- Is play fun for both of us?
- How does my animal friend communicate with me about what is pleasurable, or what is not fun?
- Do I let my animal friend take the lead during play, either initiating play or choosing the type of games we play together?
- How do I show my animal friend affection?
- If my dog companion is tied to a doghouse for long periods of time, is it possible to take him or her with me to some of the places I must go? Is the "run" long enough to allow for exercise during my absence?

SUNLIGHT

- Is my animal friend an indoor animal? If so, are there windowsills or other avenues for fresh air and sunlight that are easily accessible?
- If my animal companion is an indoor pet, do I provide natural grasses, catnip, or herbs to compensate for what he or she would forage for outdoors?

ILLNESS

- Am I available to my animal friend during illness?
- What provisions do I make for his or her comfort during these times?

EFFECTIVE DISCIPLINE

- How do I reinforce appropriate behavior with my animal friend?
- Have I been able to learn how to verbally communicate with my animal companion so that a simple yes or no is easily understood and elicits the desired response?

DOG AND CAT DENS

- Does my animal companion have a private refuge of basket, box, or den? How accessible is it? Do its cushions or padding have removable washable covers to prevent the breeding of fleas?

CHAPTER 4

Hervena

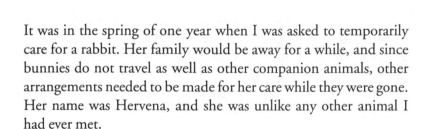

It was in the spring of one year when I was asked to temporarily care for a rabbit. Her family would be away for a while, and since bunnies do not travel as well as other companion animals, other arrangements needed to be made for her care while they were gone. Her name was Hervena, and she was unlike any other animal I had ever met.

A big, black Flemish giant with large, soft brown eyes and a quivering, curious nose, Hervena had a personality that filled a room. Never having met a rabbit before, I could not estimate her intelligence in comparison to other rabbits, but I do know that she was very bright, as inquisitive and adept as any cat or dog who had shared my life. There was little that she feared—and with good reason. Her powerful hind legs ended in thick, sharp, one-inch claws, and her hearing and eyesight, as any rabbit's, were acutely perfect. Aside from being bright, courageous, and strong, she had a loving side to her personality. She delighted in being held and combed and took great interest in anything new.

Hervena quickly became the center of attention at our house.

Her oversized cage was placed under a sunny double window in our kitchen. From this vantage point she was the center of much activity at mealtimes and dish washing. The only telephone jack in the house was in that room, and my computer, set up for schoolwork, was within view of her cage. We exchanged greetings and looks throughout the day and were never very far apart.

Evenings were our special time. With the kitchen cordoned off from the rest of the house, we would sit together on the linoleum floor for hours. Sometimes we would play with empty bath-tissue tubes. I would roll them across the floor toward her, and she would race after them, pick them up with her front teeth, and fling them across the room. She would scamper after them and repeat the tossing game. Other times, she would chase a spherical wire ball across the floor, hitting it briskly with a front paw, causing it to spin and roll, scampering after that, too. Some evenings she would nestle against my thigh as I sat with my back to a wall, reading.

Once, evening after evening, I read aloud to her Richard Adams's *Watership Down*.[1] Cover to cover it was a four-week project that resulted in a library late fine but was well worth it. That she particularly seemed to enjoy our reading time together, I had no doubt, though it would be a stretch for me to assert that she understood the story rather than simply being content with warm companionship and the rhythmic sound of my voice. But I do remember many moments, especially when reading parts of the tale in which various rabbits were experiencing one difficulty or another, that Hervena would seem especially attentive, occasionally looking up at me as I read or nuzzling even closer to my thigh.

One day a call came with the request that Hervena remain with us indefinitely. We were glad of the news. From then on, our lives together assumed a rhythm as the seasons and years passed, and life was sure and sweet. We played, scampered, and sat together looking out the back kitchen window at birds and chipmunks and squirrels. She taught me how to give rabbit massages and played with small plastic toys in her weekly warm baths. Eventually, she even learned to hold still for toenail trimming sessions, which she really did not like.

For the most part, her daily tribulations as a member of my family consisted of having to choose which organic vegetable to eat first: the kale or the burdock root, in which corner of her huge cage would the pile of hay look best, and should she grasp the wire mesh of her enclosure with her front claws, and give a big stretch to her body accompanied by a cavernous yawn—before or after another nap? On her worst day, she had the luxury of the bunny bath, a warm soak in sudsy organic shampoo, during which she rested her front paws on my forearm and gazed trustingly up at me, sometimes snuggling her whiskered nose into the crook of my arm.

Then one day, I noticed that she was not feeling well, and her stools were loose. It's always the risk we take when we say hello to someone—that we inevitably have to say good-bye. That Hervena would be an exception I had never doubted, yet I had nurtured a hope all these years that her parting would be natural, from old age. But it was not to be.

I called the clinic, and it was decided that she should be seen right away. Several tests needed to be done to gather more information. Soon the diagnosis was in.

When I arrived at the clinic the vet ushered me into the examination room with a nod of his head. An ultrasound and physical exam had revealed that the problem was not an impaction of undigested hay but a number of abscesses in Hervena's abdominal cavity and intestinal tract.

I had talked with the vet on the phone a few hours earlier and stated my reluctance to go through another euthanasia like the one three years before. This would be the first euthanasia since McTavish's, and I met this situation with a mixture of dread and a hope that this time things were going to be very different. He understood my feelings, concerns, and my request. We decided we would do this as a team, and I would be an informed participant, rather than an observer.

It was dusk on February 29, Leap Day, a very auspicious day for a rabbit. Now there was one last hurdle we would overcome together. The trust and love that we'd developed and shared over the last half decade would be the endowment that would get us through this. Thinking about all our happy times together gave me courage and peace of heart to proceed with this one last act of intentional love for her.

Together we released Hervena from her pain. He injected bit by bit a sedative into her thigh that took her deeper and deeper into subconsciousness while I held her paw, stroking her ears and telling her how much I loved her, that as in all things we had done together, this too would be all right.

Soon came the final injection. With one hand stroking her long, silky ears and the other resting on her shoulder, I felt her final breath leave her tired body. My last thoughts were happy as Hervena slipped away: Run, Hervena! Run! And as I came out into the reception room, a Beatles' song was playing on the radio:

> Here comes the sun
> Little darlin'
> Here comes the sun.
> And I say,
> It's all right.

This time things were different. I had chosen to be a participant in her assisted death process as well as in her life. I was prepared, assessed my options to help her, and made informed decisions based on the options available to us. In all matters related to my animal companions, I believe it vital to do all I can but to do no harm. I am always grateful to be present when it is time to say good-bye to them. No one should ever have to die alone. Being with them in this, their last act of living, is important to me. I need to know that they understand that my presence, based on the trust I have earned through my relationship with them, is an indication that everything will be all right. Performing this last office of friendship is always a demonstration of how much I have come to love them. It's my way of saying, We've been through much together, you and I; we've had happy times (and difficult ones), done much, been everywhere together. You were, and are, important to me. And I will go through this one last journey with you.

Despite the fact that both Hervena and her cage were no longer with us, there were times in the weeks that followed when I would hear, or would think I heard, various noises she always made. Few sounds resemble a bunny crunching on a burdock root, a good, solid whack to a water bottle, or the brisk thump of a powerful hind leg on plywood flooring.

I also discovered that the habits and behaviors that had become a part of my daily patterns of life with her were deeply ingrained. I found myself stepping over the space on the kitchen floor where the corner of her cage used to rest. Several times I automatically perused the burdock roots at the store with the intention of buying them. In these and in many other ways, Hervena was still very much with me, and each memory brought happiness as well as sadness.

The months that followed were another time of many firsts as I learned new habits and filled the now-empty time we used to share together with new activities. I learned to take good care of myself and not to push myself into new activities merely to take up the time. Each day became a time of relearning my own rhythm of life, the rhythm of life without a rabbit.

But it is because Hervena had such a wonderful life, had so many people who loved her without hesitation, that my heart, though missing her, is happy and at peace. Letting her go was sad, but it was also bearable. I know I gave her a really good life; hers was a life of opportunities, happiness, and recognition of her unique personality. And my life was made so much richer for having known and loved her.

CHAPTER 5

The Euthanasia Decision

When at the end of the road during a long illness, when recovery from an accident seems unlikely, or when old age settles in and the body tires, all humans and their animal companions come to the same crossroad: a parting of ways. Being present with death is always difficult and sad. Whether making the decision with your vet to euthanize or supporting your animal companion during a natural death process, the choice is always a difficult and at times a lonely task.

An animal companion may be helped by euthanasia, especially if the death process is accompanied by pain. What is important to consider during this time is how to minimize suffering—your animal companion's or yours.

But sorting out feelings is a difficult task when we are under stress and we are faced with tough decisions. When we truly bond with an animal, we are blessed with the gift of understanding how they are experiencing their daily realities. From countless interactions with them, we have learned to interpret successfully their reactions to daily events; we know on an intuitive level when they are happy or sad, when they feel comfortable in their bodies or are experiencing discomfort. If we have taken the time to know these precious members of our families, we are usually aware when they are physically losing ground. While this knowledge may arouse a certain sense of dread at facing these difficult decisions, we should take comfort in the fact that our animal companions are indicating their needs to us, and this can relieve us of some of the burden of the decision-making process.

It may be helpful to us, if we are feeling very confused, to talk to a veterinarian about the specific physical condition of our animal companion. Some diseases are painful in the later stages of their development, but others are not accompanied by pain or physical discomfort. A veterinarian may be a great source of information on this topic, and his or her skill and past experiences with other animals who have been in similar situations may be helpful as you consider all the options.

To euthanize or not to euthanize may be the most difficult and painful decision we are faced with in our relationship with an animal companion. It is only fair to everyone involved that we make the best decision we can make and that we act with a clear conscience when action is warranted. To do this we must give ourselves permission to gather as much information as we can; if answers are not forthcoming from one source, we can seek out other professionals who may have answers for us. No one is expected to make choices in a vacuum, nor is it wise to do so. All important decisions in our own lives and in the lives of those we love take time, and good, sound decisions are best made when we are fully informed and have taken all of the facts into account.

More difficult in the process of choosing euthanasia is sorting out whose pain will be alleviated by making this choice. There is little room for doubt if a consultation with a trusted veterinarian has made it clear that your animal companion's quality of life will be greatly reduced as the result of lingering illness or aging physiological functions. But as humans, we have come to learn that we sometimes shy away from emotional pain, and it is very human to try to delay the inevitable, even if only for a little while.

This is an important juncture in our relationships with our animal counterparts. We must have the courage and love to make the decision based only on the needs of our friend, putting our own needs aside. We must be very certain that we are not choosing euthanasia to relieve our own emotional suffering or because it is too painful to be with our animal companion during a natural, painless death process. Conversely, it is also vital that we not prolong an animal's suffering in order to postpone what we may anticipate as a personally traumatic event—being present with our animal companion during a euthanasia procedure. We must not rob our animal companions of the dignity they so justly deserve. As their loving stewards, it is our duty to assist them in their death process in an appropriate way. For their sake this means with as little pain and discomfort as possible and with love, respect, and comforting from the humans who have participated in all the events of their lives.

It is important to recognize that "all the events of their lives" includes the last event—dying. It may give us great courage and comfort to know that many of our animal companions have specifically chosen us to participate in the most important event of their lives—the last transition from one state to another—because we have attained certain qualities in our process of becoming fully human. To be so chosen may well be one of life's greatest honors. Certainly, this knowledge does little to diminish our pain of loss, but it is not necessarily meant to; there are times when learning important lessons entails suffering, and sometimes the true reward is simply a deeper understanding of the mystery of personal existence.

We may experience many emotions as we attempt to sort out for whom the euthanasia experience will or will not alleviate suffering. We may find ourselves feeling guilt at our urge to put our own emotional needs first. We may experience anger and resentment at being faced with this situation in the first place. We may find our anger and resentment directed at our animal companion's health care providers, ourselves, God or fate, or even our animal friend. It is easy to slip into denial at this stage of events, trying desperately to convince ourselves and those around us that things will get better, that we won't have to make this decision after all. We may even revert back to old thinking patterns, that our companion is "only" a dog/cat/guinea pig; that not missing time from work is more important; that we have looked forward to our upcoming vacation for months and we deserve it.

What we cannot escape is that small voice in our heart, the one that speaks to us in the quiet moments when the rest of the world is sound asleep, the one that we know to be our higher self and our connection with all that is good about being fully human. This is the voice that will speak loudly and insistently about how our actions have measured up when we have come to the end of this chapter of our life's experiences. We cannot escape our deep intuitive knowing of whether or not we have acted in accordance with our own ethics and value systems, and it is this inner voice that will lead us to choices and experiences that will free us to be who we truly are.

The key here is honesty. Such deep, uncompromising self-assessment may be painful in the short run, but these experiences, when faced head-on with courage and clear intention, will lead to spiritual growth. That such profound personal reflection should factor into our human–animal relationships may come as a surprise to some of us, but many people believe that there are no coincidences and that the animals in our lives do, in fact, choose us to be a part of their earthly, physical experience for a reason. Perhaps the reason lies in their understanding that all relationships are symbiotic partnerships in which both parties naturally assist one another in a physical, emotional, and spiritual growth process.

There are countless ordinary people who—after struggling through the decision-making process to euthanize, attending the actual event, and experiencing their emotions with raw, intense honesty—assert that their reward for intentional participation was more of the same. Astonishingly, these people reflect that they have had subsequent opportunities to assist other humans and animals in the experience of the death process, and invariably, these same people emphasize that each death they attend is something of a blessing, a gift of seeing into another realm.

Other people believe that being present at the natural or assisted death of an animal has somehow made them better humans than they were before. They say that the experience has made them emotionally stronger and spiritually more peaceful, providing closure to their relationship with their animal companion and insight into their own inevitable experience of dying. But whatever the changes we experience as the result of seeing our animal companions through the last event of their lives, no one can argue with the fact that such an experience is unique.

While euthanasia is a topic that your veterinarian is skilled in dealing with, and equipped to handle in a painless, dignified way, the decision between euthanasia and a natural death must be made by you and you alone. The bond between you and your animal companion may be a source of strength that will help you decide which choice is appropriate for both of you. Be sure to give yourself time to make this important decision. Other family members may also have feelings about this issue and may want to offer their thoughts and support. If appropriate, you may wish to discuss the options available or make the decision together.

The more information you gather about the physical, emotional, and spiritual needs of your animal companion, the easier your decision will be. Your veterinarian is your greatest ally in terms of physical and medical information that may aid you in your choice.

Some appropriate and common questions to ask your veterinarian may include:

- Is euthanasia the right choice for my animal companion? When is the right moment in his or her disease or aging process, and what are the signs or symptoms that will indicate that the moment has come? If I choose euthanasia, will my animal companion's life be shortened unnecessarily?
- What exactly does euthanasia entail? Will it be painful? What drugs might be used, and how will they be administered? How long will the procedure take? What are the veterinarian's previous experiences with euthanasia?
- Can family members be present, and can it take place in a location other than the veterinarian's office, such as our home or a place that we associate with happy times together?
- If choosing a natural death for my animal companion, what might be the natural progression of the disease? Will he or she experience pain? What quality of life can be expected during the time that remains? How much nursing care will he or she need for me to be fully supportive? Will it be necessary for me to take time off from work or to rearrange my schedule?

If you are comfortable with the decision to euthanize and have chosen a veterinarian to perform this service, then you have an understanding friend who is on your side. If you do not have a veterinarian and are considering this option, you may wish to talk with several veterinarians before making an appointment for euthanasia. In either case, a preliminary discussion will give you an idea of a particular veterinarian's methods of assisted death and will provide you with an opportunity to state your own needs and the needs of your animal companion.

Never hesitate to get to know a veterinarian in order to be sure that he or she agrees that euthanasia is more than just a medical procedure. It is never just a medical procedure. It is the last interaction that you will have with someone whom you have come to love and who loves you in turn. If you are uncertain about whether a particular veterinarian views euthanasia as an act of love and kindness to be performed with dignity, compassion, and respect, expand your search for a veterinarian who does. For many of us, parting from our loved ones is very painful; it is unnecessary to add regret to our grief.

Some veterinarians will perform euthanasia on a "drop-off" basis; if you choose, you need not be present. But experience has shown that, unless you are very certain in this choice, it may be wise in the long run to carefully reevaluate this decision. Grief is often hard enough to bear without the added burden of remorse. In the event that you wish to be present, many veterinarians encourage human companions to actually hold their animal friend during this procedure. In any case, do choose a veterinarian who is sensitive to both your needs and the needs of your animal companion.

CHAPTER 6

Human Grief at the Loss of an Animal Companion

Being with our animal companions as they go through their death processes is probably the most loving and caring thing we can do for them in their remaining time with us. It is an act of great courage and compassion and can be a source of great peace in our healing process of loss.

Many people will notice a bond of trust in their relationship with their animal friend. The nexus between humans and the animals in their lives often rivals that between humans. Countless stories abound of dogs and cats rescuing their people from fires, accidents, and other mishaps. Horses have the particular distinction of bringing an injured person home on their backs, and many equestrians maintain that there is more to this action than returning to the safety of the barn and the waiting feed bin. Although they are a species well known for their independence, cats that have been unexpectedly or accidently separated from their human families have been known to travel hundreds of miles to reunite with them. Such deep and heart-centered bonds develop gradually over months and years as we come to understand every nuance of their intricate personalities. Often these unions may serve as a guide through the journey toward death.

Death is a process rather than an event; it rarely happens in a few moments but evolves over time: hours, days, or weeks. You will, of course, want to see that your animal companion is provided with warmth, quiet, and as much comfort as possible. You may wish to hold your animal companion or stroke it or offer reassuring words in a soothing tone of voice. What is important in this part of your journey with your animal friend are your emotions, feelings, and intuition. Give yourself permission to listen to that higher intelligence that we all have.

Whatever you choose to do will be up to you, a personal matter between you and your friend. Let your heart connection with your animal companion be your guide through this process and know that whatever comes naturally will be the right gesture. Be present, take your time, moment by moment, heartbeat by heartbeat.

Some families of animal companions choose to have special days of memorial for their parted animal friends. In addition to the immediate family members, such gatherings may consist of extended family members, other animals within the family, and previous families of the animal who has died. It is a time of healing and remembrance for all who knew and loved this special friend. Memorial services could include a variety of ceremonies such as planting a memorial tree, a hike along a trail especially favored by a dog or horse, a picnic in a meadow favored by the cat who has died, or planting a carrot patch in the shape of a rabbit.

After being present during the death process of an animal companion and conducting whatever memorial service we feel is appropriate for honoring him or her, we may be overwhelmed by many feelings. We become aware, quite suddenly, that all the activity has stopped and our lives are filled with a stillness that at times feels almost unbearable. What we do not quite understand at first is that we have already been going through the initial stages of grief and loss as we loved and comforted our friend in his or her last days. Sometimes the later stages of the grief process may take us by surprise. If you feel overwhelmed, don't isolate yourself. Grief counseling may be available to you from your veterinarian, or he or she may be able to recommend someone professionally trained in this area or know of a local group that meets to discuss the grieving process.

All experiences of loss, including grieving the death of a loved one, entail the same stages. Individuals may go through the stages of grief in succession or may revert back to a previous stage at any point in the process, beginning again from that repeated step. The steps of loss are also referred to as the steps of healing. Everyone heals from loss at his or her own rate and taking a year or more to go through this process is not uncommon. Elisabeth Kübler-Ross pioneered work in the field of human psychology and wrote at length on the stages of grief and loss in her book *On Death And Dying.*[1] Kübler-Ross's theories and work are applicable to us all because all living things die and we are all inevitably going to experience the transition from life to death, whether our own or someone else's. To be aware of the stages of grief and loss prior to an actual experience may enrich our journey and lessen our feelings of fear and isolation.

At many junctures in my life, when coping with loss, I reread Kübler-Ross's important writings on the topic of death and dying. I have experienced the stages of this emotional journey in the same way as she lists them in her writings of clinical observations: denial, anger, bargaining, blame, depression, and acceptance. What follows is a list of the stages that Kübler-Ross outlined in her work with my interpretation of them from my own experiences, other people's shared accounts, and what I have learned from counselors and participants in grief-support groups.

DENIAL is practical as a temporary armor against fear and pain. It is a normal self-preservation response to extremely stressful situations or ones in which we may feel we are not ready to cope. Denial may occur on more than just our mental level of being; our physical, emotional, and psychic bodies may also resist change that triggers fear and pain. We may find ourselves doing tasks or daily routines that no longer apply to our ailing companions, such as reaching for the leash when our animal no longer cares to go for a walk. We may become temporarily confused when we find that our emotions are no longer appropriate for the current situation.

One woman reported a feeling of impatience when her dog, who was stricken with bone cancer, could no longer keep up during their morning run together. Her impatience stemmed not so much from anger with her dog, or resentment at her dog's new handicap, but from a deep sense of loss that her new daily schedule with her friend was evidence of change;

she was feeling rushed headlong into a changing future, a future in which she would have to say good-bye.

On a psychic level, we may find that our extrasensory perception of our animal's emotional state is no longer clearly defined. We may truly have difficulty sensing how our animal friend is feeling on an emotional level. This may be because we are grappling with our own roiling emotions, frightening or painful new feelings we may not want to experience. Other times we may find ourselves experiencing an absence of emotions as our only defense: emotional numbness can protect us from emotional over-load. In these moments, when we cannot possibly bear our own emotional responses, it is understandable that we are also incapable of perceiving another's emotional state. Love is a healing balm in this stage of loss; self-love allows us to love another and frees us to experience the miraculous transformation we call dying.

ANGER is a natural consequence when our normal defense reaction of denial no longer protects us from painful situations that we are unable to change. It may be useful for us to understand that anger is a normal sur-vival mechanism, alerting us that our boundaries of perceived personal safety have been breached.

Anger is built into our biological construct in order to ensure physical survival. When we become frightened, it is a normal human response for fear to evolve into anger, which in turn speeds up our physiological and biochemical processes; adrenaline rushes into our blood system so that we can run faster, lift more, and summon all our reserves of strength to escape from that which threatens our physical safety. Situations that threaten us emotionally are no less stressful or detrimental than those that threaten us physically, and our biochemical responses are the same.

Rage, envy, and resentment are the siblings of anger and are also nor-mal emotions. Sometimes we may find ourselves angry at the loved one who is ill, feeling resentful that the situation at hand is an interruption in our once ordered and peaceful existence. We may feel burdened at the prospect of long consultations with animal health care providers when there is already no spare time in our schedules. We may feel overwhelmed by the bills that suddenly flood in as we try to meet the new medical needs of our animal companion. Often enough we feel that there are never enough hours in the day to do all the things required of us, and now we must face the stress of adding the role of hospice worker to our increasingly demanding lives. What was once happy time spent with our animal companion is now devoted to an endless list of things related to our animal companion's care and comfort. While we still relate to our companion with love and tenderness no matter what activity fills our time together, we may find ourselves longing for those carefree days before illness arrived.

It is important to remember that feelings are just feelings, no matter how irrational or shocking they may seem. Patience and self-love are very helpful during this stage of grief or healing. Take time out to sit quietly, even for five minutes. Breathe, with no other intention than to feel the breath come in and give strength and go out, taking with it accumulated stress. Be present. A moment is a very long time.

BARGAINING is the normal reaction we experience when our anger cannot be focused into a specific action that will change a situation and lessen our pain. We bargain with everyone from God or fate or the universe to health care providers, seeking the one solution that will give us what we truly want. This too is a natural emotion. When bargaining fails, we sometimes get angry again.

BLAME is the natural progression of our emotions when anger and bargaining fail and serves as a temporary escape from our own sense of powerlessness. It has to be someone's fault, right? When we have carefully taken stock of everyone's role, and no one else seems to be at fault, we can always resort to blaming ourselves. In this stage, it is easy to become burdened with guilt and self-persecution or to boomerang back into anger or even denial.

It is important to remember that no one is to blame—death is as much a part of life as living. At this point it is very necessary to love ourselves and to seek comfort and understanding from other people with whom we feel safe and respected. When we have acted from our hearts and each action has been attended with compassion and love, we must remind ourselves that we have acted with the highest integrity. We have done our best, and our pain is a reminder that we have been fully human during the process of illness or death of our animal friend.

DEPRESSION results from suppressing our feelings. We are physically and emotionally drained, and we just don't want to feel any more. We've been through a hurricane of emotions, and any more feelings seem too much to bear. Loss of physical energy coupled with the personal knowledge that we are not going to get what we wanted can make us feel hollow and exhausted.

Just as it is helpful to remind ourselves of the tools of good self-care when we are experiencing blame, depression will also yield to a regimen of healthy habits. Eating regular, well-balanced meals; adhering to a sleeping schedule, even if we are unable to sleep through the night; practicing personal hygiene (a shower or the simple act of washing your face induces a feeling of refreshment); and adequate amounts of fresh air, exercise, and recreation time with friends and family are all routines that will help to keep our bodies from succumbing to loneliness and exhaustion.

ACCEPTANCE is the final stage of grieving or healing and finds us in a place of moving onward from the initial stages of our journey. We realize that although we have been through a natural process, it has been a difficult one. Here we may begin to feel the strength we have gained from our experience. A sense of release may be felt as another chapter of our lives begins. Acceptance may not be a permanent stage—we may find ourselves reexperiencing anger, blame, or depression. In a true stage of acceptance, we may still feel deep sadness for a very long time, but our feelings are now bearable and balanced with happy memories.

Finally accepting that our loved one is gone does not mean that we no longer miss our companion. Acceptance may simply mean that we acknowledge that we did the best we could under very difficult circumstances, even though we still feel a very deep sense of loss.

❧

If you have not been told so before, the death of a beloved animal friend is as heartbreaking as the death of any other family member.[2] You are saying good-bye to someone whom you have loved and have been loved by in turn. Likely you shared many happy and companionable moments together; you laughed and cried, played and struggled. The loss of such a friend and companion hurts—there is no way around it—and feelings of sadness, loss, and grief are appropriate and part of the healing process. Talk to your friends about your loss, without shame and guilt. Find other people who have experienced the same types of loss in their own lives and compare stories. Join a grief counseling group. Feel free to call a previous family of your animal companion and share the news of his or her passing; you will be surprised that other people have loved this friend as you have and will grieve as you do.

Lastly, display in your home those family photographs that include your animal friend, and remember the happy times, the special times you shared together. You were important in the life of your beloved companion; you made a mark in his or her life and gave it the special dimension of loving friendship.

CHAPTER 7

Cat

March winds skirted the houses on our block. Rain threatened again, as it had for the last four days, and looking out the kitchen window I wondered if the sun, when it poked through the clouds, would squint its eyes at its own brightness. Gray. All the world seemed gray, and I longed for the smell of green growing things and the songs of birds. The floorboards squeaked as I walked back toward the other end of the house, and beyond the grate of board on board came another sound, that of a loud, sharp noise. I instantly froze, in order to identify this strange sound, but all was still and the sound did not come again. It was a new experience for us to be living in an urban area, and we were still getting used to the myriad noises that humans make in close habitation with one another. I dismissed the clamor as another that I would soon learn to identify and went on with my day.

The next afternoon, I got a call from an acquaintance of mine. He had a cat, he said, who needed a place to stay. While my work with animals frequently brings calls for help that include finding new homes for displaced animals, there was an underlying urgency in his voice that made me pause and ask for more details. The story he told me was unusual at best, and when I began to piece the particulars of the situation together, I too felt anxious. A close friend of my acquaintance's had been suffering from a terminal illness for several years, and he had exhausted all possibilities for a successful treatment. The poor fellow, in pain and despair, had committed suicide the day before. This event had taken place in the house directly behind mine. I remembered the sharp, loud noise I'd heard the previous day and wondered if that unfamiliar sound had any connection. My acquaintance went on to relate how a cat had been left in the wake of these events, and how he was left instructions to provide for her in the event that something should happen to her person. Unfortunately, my acquaintance could not have an animal companion in his rented apartment, and he was calling me for help.

As it was, my own lease stated that our animal allotment was limited to two, and we were full up. I said I would make some calls to try to find a temporary housing situation for her and signed off. After several calls, I made contact with another friend who was willing to take this abandoned cat into her home. But, she stressed, it would be only temporary, and she could not guarantee how her own resident cat would react to a visitor.

Two more days passed before I was allowed to enter the next-door apartment to rescue her. While this deferment troubled me, I had no choice but to accept it, and I tried to focus on the positive aspect that I would soon help her. I arrived with transport carrier in hand and nerves braced for any outcome. What greeted me at the door was a riotous confusion of disorder and chaos.

The entire apartment looked as though it had been lived in for a long time; objects were scattered everywhere, with no apparent order or purpose in mind. The thing that particularly unnerved me was the profusion of rubber bands. They were everywhere, covering every available surface, scattered over every floor throughout the apartment, and they seemed to number in the thousands.

The reason that this singular jumble alarmed me was that I had seen firsthand the harm a swallowed rubber band can do to a cat, and I had made it a point in my own housekeeping practice to never leave these dangerous objects where my cats could get them. Fastidious about this aspect of animal care, I had extended a housewide ban on other objects of similar shape. For years we had forgone tinsel as a Christmas tree decoration; we gave up the use of thin paper-covered wire strips as plastic bag closures and tied the bags closed instead; and we all made it a point to never leave string or dental floss laying about but twisted discards into small knots and placed them in the bottom of the trash bucket. That this cat had not succumbed to temptation amazed me, especially since there were thousands of rubber bands all within easy reach.

Amid the profusion of clutter, I heard a small rustle coming from a side room. I walked toward the sound, which instantly escalated into a frantic, scrambling noise and saw the tip of a very fluffy, black, plumelike tail disappear around a corner. I realized in a flash that this was a very frightened animal. My task was not going to be an easy one. My acquaintance caught my gaze, gestured for me to sit in a chair, and placed his finger to his lips in mute instruction for me to be silent.

It was a full ten minutes before her curiosity overtook her fright and I saw, out of the corner of my eye, a very pretty cat face peer around the door frame of the side room. It was a sweet face, framed in flowing white hair with a black mask over eyes, forehead, and ears; the mask extended up over the crown of her head and down her shoulders, like a hood, and took up again just below her shoulder blades and continued the length of her tail. But for all her pretty sweetness, the yellow eyes that stared back at me were huge. Shocked, haunted, and panicked, they gazed at me with terror.

In a whisper, I asked my friend where the cat had been when her person died. He shrugged his shoulders in a gesture indicating that he did not know. Was she inside when her person was found, I mouthed. An affirmative nod. I silently counted on my fingers the days that had passed since I heard the odd noise. Four. She'd been here during the event, and it was now four days later. I looked at the cat and she looked back at me, and I realized with a pang that this animal was likely suffering from post-traumatic stress disorder. Intuitively, I sensed that this was going to be far more difficult than I had originally thought, and I also began to comprehend that my relationship with this cat was only at a starting point.

After several quiet attempts to pick her up, my friend cornered her and from there we got her into the transport carrier in as gentle a way as possible. Once inside, she settled down, as if relieved by the security the smallness of the carrier provided.

Within a short amount of time we arrived at her temporary home, and there she was whisked into an enclosed porch area in the back of the house. I left a flower essence to be given to her at intervals throughout the evening and next day as well as a few doses of Aconite and some cat food I'd brought along.

The call came on the second day of her stay. She'd been bullied unmercifully by the resident cat ever since she arrived. It was simply a matter of territory and complicated rules of feline pride behavior. Despite her temporary guardian's every effort, the situation was out of control; she had spent the last thirty-six hours hiding in the undercovering of a box spring mattress and had not come out even once to use a litter box. For everyone's peace of mind, for safety, and the pleasure of a good night's sleep, it was time for her to go.

I arrived with transport carrier in tow, wondering how on earth (or in heaven) I, a complete stranger, would manage to corral her and get her into it. I needn't have worried; she went easily, almost gratefully.

We arrived home shortly afterward and began our ritual of getting acquainted and setting safe perimeters for her to settle in. With the door closed, my room became her safe haven for the next few days. She had her own litter box, food and water bowls, and a "binky" of socks to bat around. I had learned from Bruno that two socks folded on themselves made a very good, soft toy in a pinch. This, in dog circles, is called a binky and usually comprises a ball tied into the toe of an old sock. But I didn't have a ball, and I would not dream of giving her one of the toys belonging to our resident cat, Acacia. So she had a makeshift binky, and it needed to be good enough.

I began to observe her behavior in an effort to unravel the mystery of her trauma. I would need to figure out how to help her heal emotionally from her ordeal. I also began to make small headway in calming her and provided every opportunity for her to learn to trust again, but it was slow going.

On the third night, she came out from behind the laundry basket in the corner of my bedroom and sat crouched on the far corner of the futon. After a half an hour of "not looking at her," I reached out a tentative hand. At this, she flew back to the protective cover of the basket. In the morning, however, I awoke to find her sleeping on the foot of the bed. We were making progress!

Still later, at dinnertime that day, she allowed me to stroke her head. It wasn't a full stroke, mind you, but a brief touch followed by a quick ducking away from my outstretched hand. But again, we were beginning to get acquainted.

The binky was also getting its full share of attention. In the evenings when I settled into bed, I would toss it to her. She, with feline ferociousness, would snatch it out of the air with her claws and proceed to ravish it in the most aggressive manner. Kicking, biting, and snarling at the limp and passive ball of socks, she seemed to be taking out her pent-up anger and frustration. After a moment she would stop, thrust it from her, and sit panting, gasping, and growling at it, her eyes mere slits and ears folded back in rage and fury. I suspected that this was very good therapy for her, and this aspect of our work together lasted almost a month. Then I noted that she began to play with it in a much more normal fashion.

On the fourth day after she arrived at our home, I opened the bedroom door and left it open. It was time for Acacia to get a look at who was skulking around in my room. This was a very difficult moment for all of us. Acacia had slept with me for a long time, and because she is a Natrum muriaticum constitution, being displaced brought up her abandonment issues once again. With the advent of her aroused emotional state, she began licking and chewing compulsively and obsessively at her skin and was now "a wreck," as we often called her. Try as I might, no amount of comfort or attention assuaged her injured feelings. Soon after the arrival of the new cat, my son gladly let her sleep in his bed, and this helped, along with a few doses of her remedy.

At the doorway of my now-opened room, green eyes locked on yellow eyes, and a mad scramble to hiding places ensued. In moments there was not a cat to be seen—or heard. I left the door open and went about washing up the morning dishes. Within moments, a frenzied and savage howling came from the hall by my room.

"Ladies!" I shouted. "Please!" At this, I could hear cat claws scrabbling to gain purchase on hardwood floors, followed by the sound of small, running feet. Then silence. Total and utter silence.

Acacia peered at me from under a chair as I walked to the hall. I reached down and picked her up, giving her a reassuring hug in the process. She squirmed to get out of my arms in a gesture that clearly spoke of deep, unforgiving resentment at my betrayal. I put her down and went into the bedroom to assess the new damage.

Glaring accusingly, yellow eyes scrutinized me from behind the basket. All attempts at making up failed. I partly closed the door so that it was open only a crack and went to the phone.

The first order of business was learning her name. I had been given her veterinary records, which dated back two years. They were incomplete; her name was missing. All that the records indicated was her species: cat. I soon learned that this was actually her name; the mistake had occurred in filling in the blank spaces on the form. In the tradition of the Welsh, her previous person had named her by her species. The Welsh often call their horse "Horse," their dog "Dog," and very often name a cat "Cat." Why they do so remains a mystery, yet it is a cultural habit that has lasted generations.

So, Cat it was. And I began using her name that very minute. I walked into my room and said, "Cat." At this, she perked up her ears and came sidling over to me. A brief brush to my jeans with the side of her tail, a rub of the whiskers. I was being marked, acknowledged, and thanked.

Throughout the day, I called her by name, and the response was a welcome sight. She would move toward me, often backing away before making actual contact, but again, we were making remarkable progress. At times, she seemed almost to smile. My heart was glad.

In the late afternoon I called her name from the kitchen, and she appeared in the doorway. Coaxing her from the safety of the doorframe, she came to my outstretched hand. Acacia glared at this new development from under the chair. Then in true cat fashion, according to all the rules of the cat pride, Cat did a very normal thing. She marched herself to the back door of the kitchen, spun around, lifted her tail with a shudder, and sprayed the doorway. My spirits fell. Not only was this unacceptable to Acacia, it was very bad indeed for the status of my lease.

Over the next few days, in between washing and scrubbing the back door area, I talked with my friend Nena, who is an animal communicator. She said that she would talk to Cat long-distance and discuss several points with her. The first would be about how she was doing emotionally and how she was adjusting to, or thinking about, her new family. The second would be why she was spraying in our apartment, and what I could do to resolve the situation. Nena also agreed to communicate with Acacia, to see how she was coping with the new situation in our lives and to ask if there was anything we humans could do to make things easier for her.

The actual communication event with Cat was one of the most unusual things I have ever witnessed. As had become her afternoon custom, Cat was sitting on top of the kitchen cabinets that extended almost to the ceiling, with her back to the corner, when the communication occurred. I saw her up there moments before and took no particular notice. But out of the corner of my eye, I saw that she was holding her head at a peculiar angle, as though listening to someone whisper in her ear.

Glancing at the clock, I watched in fascination as Cat continued to do this for several minutes, eyes closed and ear cocked at an odd angle, an expression of deep concentration on her face. After a bit, she opened her eyes and looked directly into mine. After a few moments of this, she resumed holding her head to the side, with her eyes closed and a thoughtful expression on her face. Then, without so much as a warning, she yawned, placed her chin on her outstretched paws, and fell instantly asleep.

Later, when I again spoke with Nena, she related that she communicated with Cat at the very time when I observed her odd behavior. She further told me that Cat had stated that she was OK with being with us; it was neither good nor bad, she was merely accepting of her new situation. As to the spraying of the kitchen door, the action was being done, as I had guessed, for territorial reasons; she needed to mark a place to claim it as her own. What could I do to help resolve the situation? It was very important, Cat indicated, for me to make up my mind about whether or not she was going to be allowed to stay with us.

This was a real shock to me. In no way had I suggested to Nena that I was still undecided about keeping Cat and making her a permanent member of our family! There was no possible way for her to have known that—unless she had come upon the information by way of someone other than me. The only other person I shared my living space with was my son and, of course, the two cats and our rabbit.

What else, I wanted to know, could I do? Nena stated that I not only needed to make up my mind but I needed to state my decision out loud to Cat. This would reassure her if it was a positive decision in her favor; if it was not, at least she would know where she stood.

But what about the spraying, I wanted to know; this was the real problem, no? No. The real problem, Nena insisted, was that I had not bothered to try to discuss these issues with Cat. I had been operating in a vacuum, assuming that what I saw was what she had to tell me. What she really had to tell me was that she felt lonely, displaced, and adrift on an uncertain future. Above all else, she needed reassurance, and I was not meeting her needs.

Superficially, I thought this whole idea fantastic, unbelievable, pure fiction. Yet, a still, small voice inside me knew that all she was saying was true. I had been operating in my own small world, a world of human interpretation. True, I had done the best that my humanity allowed, but here was a challenge for me to go further, to test new horizons, to suspend my present belief systems and experience the world in a very different way. Was I ready?

I took the plunge and instantly made the decision that if anyone was going to help this cat, it had to be me. No one else had come forward. Providence, God, Kismet had put us together, and for good or for bad, it seemed that we were destined to be a family. Yes, I said. She is here to stay. What must I do to get her to stop spraying?

Nena had asked Cat this very question. Cat told her that it would be very helpful to her if I would gently remind her that she did not need to spray in order to announce to everyone that this was now her home. Cat went on to state that once a cat begins this behavior, it quickly becomes a habit, but verbal reminders can help a cat stop the behavior.

My rational mind took over once again. Now weren't we stretching this a bit thin? It was one thing for me to acquiesce to the reality of the shadowy world of interspecies communication; it was a step I took haltingly, but I did it. It was another leap for me to accept that missing information regarding my indecision about keeping this cat had been communicated from the cat in question to an animal communicator nearly one hundred miles distant. But this too, in defiance of a logical explanation, I had accepted. Reservedly and skeptically, but accepted nonetheless. Now I was being asked to believe that the solution for what I perceived as the root problem was logically and rationally coming from the cat herself. Balderdash, hogwash, and puppy biscuits! But what other solution was presenting itself? None that I could see. And besides, I had nothing to lose, except perhaps my present map of reality, which was being redrawn minute by minute. I decided to give it a try.

I sought out Cat and found her lying on the futon in my room. I sat down and, feeling extremely foolish, began a long monologue. "Look," I said. "We want you here, really we do. You're very sweet and all that, and I realize you've been through a terrible ordeal. It's too bad that your friend is no longer around to care for you, and we will gladly take you into our family, but there's this little problem, you see." I looked over at her, hoping for some support, some response. She merely lay there with her eyes closed, looking as though I might be interrupting the most important nap of her life.

I took a deep breath, gave thanks that no one else was at home, and continued. "It's the spraying, you see. I'm going to get in a lot of trouble if it continues, and it's an awful lot of work to keep it cleaned up. Since you're going to stay with us forever and ever," I added encouragingly, "you really don't need to do it anymore. Instead, why don't you establish some territory by staking out the other rooms, barring the one Acacia sleeps in, of course, and find some other places you'd like to nap other than my bed or the top of the kitchen cabinets? How about if we put your food and water bowls in the kitchen with the others, and your litter box in the bath-room? That will naturally increase your territory and make it clear to ev-eryone (meaning Acacia) that the entire living space is yours to share with the rest of us."

At this juncture she appeared entirely and soundly asleep. Not wishing to further disturb her and having covered all the main issues, I quietly left the room. This was going to be an interesting experiment, I thought to myself. Already I had gotten amazing results: I had facilitated a very restful nap.

The actual results came later that evening as I was doing the washing up after dinner. I'd been standing at the kitchen sink, wrestling with a large, unwieldy pan, when I became aware of Cat sitting on the floor be-hind me. I dried my hands on a towel and turned fully around and said hello. She looked at me, got up, and began wandering around the room. After a few minutes of this, she wandered toward the back door, backed up to it, lifted her tail, and looked expectantly at me. My immediate reaction was to rush forward, but I managed to hold myself in check.

"No, Cat," I said aloud. "You don't have to do that." She immediately put her tail down and walked away, without so much as a backward glance at me or the door. That I was astounded is an understatement. This behavior, reminder, and response were repeated numerous times over the next two days. We made rapid progress. When I saw her heading in the general direction of the door, all I had to do was whisper a soft "no," and she would turn around in midstride and head elsewhere. And it was not a case of going off to find another place to spray because I never saw her spray again, nor did I ever find evidence of other markings. That was simply the end of it.

A whole new world was opening before my eyes. I had known all my life that my cats understood me, but this was a very different, intimate, and immediate level of communication that I was witnessing. To have information from my cats relayed to me through another individual was a new vista in my perception about the awareness and thought processes of cats and about ways we can communicate with them.

Nena had also been in communication with Acacia. This was not an event that I was privileged to witness, though what the communicator had told me about their "conversation" was no less astonishing.

It seemed that Acacia was upset because she had lost her favorite sleeping place. In fact, she even liked Cat and did not see her as a threat, except for the loss of her rightful place to sleep by my side. I took this news personally. Just as Nena had no way of knowing that I had been undecided about keeping Cat, she also had no way of knowing that Acacia's sleeping place had been usurped by a stranger. I also took it personally because I had broken one of my own rules: when taking in a new cat always, always, always make sure to put the resident cat first in all things.

As an honorary member of several cat prides, I have upheld the feline rules of trust, fealty, and hierarchy within these relationships. I knew better than to allow a new cat to take over any thing or any place that was the personal property of any of my resident cats—and yet I had done it. I did it because Cat needed a great deal of help in healing from her emotional trauma and also because, at the time, the only room available to her was my own, and I was the only person in her life who had extended a hopeful hand of friendship. But my transgression had a profound impact on Acacia; she was chewing at her skin in an even more obsessive way, and her stools were loose again, in true Natrum muriaticum expression.

Years before, I had taken her in as a kitten lost in an early spring sleet storm. She was very ill and suffering from frostbite and salmonella as the result of eating from a compost pile. With the help of her constitutional remedy and large bottles of electrolyte solution, I had nursed her through a very frightening illness of spiking fevers, copious diarrhea, and what seemed to be indifference to life. We had bonded during that time; she learned to trust and embrace the joy of living, and we were fast and uncompromising friends. Now I had broken her trust by letting another cat sleep in her bed, and not only that, I had also made it impossible for her to defend her sleeping place by keeping the door to it closed.

I knew our bonds ran deep, and on this surety, made ready to right my wrong. I gave her a dose of Natrum muriaticum, and for the next two nights, let Cat have the run of the apartment while Acacia and I slept together in my son's room, since he was away visiting a friend.

The first night as I settled in to sleep, she refused to come up on the bed. But soon, longing for comfort overcame hurt feelings, and she snuggled in beside me. I have a vague memory of that night: a warm bit of cat nestled into the crook of my neck, purring loudly and consistently throughout the hours as if to tell the world she had finally come home.

The next day found her acting very much her old self again. Gone was the needling clinginess and bids for attention that culminated in angry rebuffs; no skin or fur was chewed or obsessively groomed; every greeting was answered with a joyful trill and an affectionate rub.

The second night we curled up together at once, I reading for a while, she simply being present and happy. We slept the night away, blissful in the comfort of each other's companionship.

The following day, my son returned home, and that night, Acacia went skipping into his room at her accustomed bedtime. I looked in on them before going to bed myself, and found them snuggled up together, both sound asleep.

While things were settling down for Acacia, Cat seemed to be having new problems. I had noticed when she first came to stay with us that she was exceedingly jumpy at the slightest noise. This did not surprise me because her previous person had committed suicide with a revolver, and in view of the fact that their shared apartment was very small, she must have been within short range of the explosion. But another development had also ensued. Every time I attempted to pick her up, she would panic. This in and of itself was not unusual, and I attributed it to her fear of strangers.

My acquaintance told me that the only person who could get near her had been her previous person. She had originally been a stray, and it had taken him months to convince her to even enter the foyer leading to his apartment so he could feed her. It had taken another few months before she would let him touch even the top of her head in a passing gesture of friendship. Even after she willingly came inside to his living space, she would never let visitors approach her.

The panic she exhibited when being picked up did not bother me as much as what occurred when I then tried to put her down. She would ineffectually flail her forelegs, scrambling for any footing in what seemed a wild attempt to keep from falling. She even seemed terrified at falling off furniture. Although she made her daily sojourn up to the privacy of the cabinet tops, and going up was a graceful movement to observe, getting down again seemed an exercise in terror for her. Crashing was the way she would land, and once paws touched whatever surface they came in contact with, everything within striking distance would go flying out behind her as she raced to the safety of the futon.

I set about figuring out what her homeopathic remedy could be. Sometimes, when pondering a case that has an odd, rare, or peculiar symptom as a component, I begin with that peculiar symptom. "Dread of downward motion" was listed in the repertory of symptoms, followed by a single remedy: Borax. In William Boericke's *Materia Medica* under the heading Borax, I found the following mental symptoms of the Borax individual listed:

> Excessive anxiety, especially from movements which have a downward motion; being carried, rocked or traversing down stairs all bring on anxiety. There is a look of extreme anxiety on the face during the downward movement, jerks and throws the hands up as if afraid of falling. Excessively nervous and easily frightened; reactive to sudden noises. Violent fright from the firing of a gun, even when it is fired at a distance; fear of loud noises, like thunder.[1]

I needed to look no further, the peculiar nervous symptoms of this remedy fit her perfectly.

At bedtime that night I gave her a dose of 30c. She did not wish me to place any of the pilules in her mouth, so I dissolved a dose in a bit of milk and gave her a bit to drink. She didn't drink it. Instead, she made digging motions on the floor around the bowl, marking the area with scent from the scent glands between the pads of her front feet. Marking her food bowls and other possessions has become one of her characteristic personality traits. I finally resorted to giving her the milk dilution with an eye dropper, an experience we both resisted. As I settled into bed, nursing my bandage-covered scratch, I noticed she was already asleep, an indication that the remedy and potency were both right and already working.

In the morning I went about my usual routine, dishing out homemade cat food and heating water for tea. Cat came sleepily into the kitchen with me and jumped onto the counter in front of me. Without thinking, I picked her up and gave her an enthusiastic hug. Acacia came galloping into the room in her usual morning frenzy, and as I put Cat down on the floor, I noticed an odd thing. She simply got down; no fuss, no struggle, no wild flailing of paws and scrambling to hook into my sweatshirt. We had achieved a huge measure of success, and more healing would come with repeated doses of Borax when they were indicated by a milder return of emotional symptoms.

It is now more than a year later, and we truly are a family. I look back on Cat's ordeal and realize that her loss was not expressed as grief but as fear from the trauma she witnessed. Sometimes she sits in the window of my bedroom and looks out to the yard that used to be hers. At these times she seems pensive and sad and refuses to respond to the sound of my voice or my small attempts at comfort. I wonder if she misses her person; if she waits there watching, to see if he will appear. I wonder if she remembers him and the times she would come home and he would open the door to her waiting supper. Perhaps I will never know.

What I do know is that, at least for now, we live here, next door to where she used to live. And while she lives only a few hundred feet away from her old home, she has come far. She is healing, and she is with people who dearly love her and who will continue to support her in her healing process. When it is time for us to move on, we will, and she will have a new yard to look out on. We hope it will be a quiet place in the country, far from barking dogs and spinning car tires. Then she will be an outdoor cat once again, and she and Acacia can explore a whole new world together.

CHAPTER 8

Animals Grieve for the Loss of Their Friends, Too

Many people wonder if animals grieve when they have experienced the loss of another animal within the family. Most animals who live together within the social group of a family share a deep bond of reciprocal friendship, sometimes borne out of the fact that they are littermates, but always in some kind of relationship to one another. We simply have no way of knowing if animals, like humans, go through the stages of grief and healing, although psychics who communicate telepathically with animals assert that they do indeed undergo the same process.[1] After the death of one animal companion, we may find ourselves noticing changed behavior in the animals that remain in our families, and in these changed behaviors, we may notice a similarity to our own process of grieving.

Animals who have experienced a loss in a family group may exhibit behaviors that resemble grief in a variety of ways.[2] Some may search endlessly for the absent family member or seek out additional attention from their human companions. Others may exhibit changes in their eating or sleeping habits, mope around, or simply act depressed.

During this stressful time for our surviving animal companions, we can be attentive to their extra needs when they exhibit changes in their normal behavior. Just as good self-care is vital as we humans move through the stages of loss or grief, so too, our other animal companions are greatly comforted by extra attention, exercise, plenty of rest, a nutritious diet, and balanced amounts of peace and quiet and structured activity.

Other supportive measures that we may find helpful are the homeopathic remedies normally associated with symptoms of stress, anger, loss, and depression.[3] It is important, however, when choosing a homeopathic remedy to alleviate emotional and mental symptoms, that we are very objective and specific about the emotional state of the individual exhibiting symptoms. Some homeopaths believe that symptoms, whether physical, mental, emotional, or psychic, are not true representations of the essence of an individual being. They believe, rather, that symptoms are survival-based adaptive responses to stress. Further, many homeopaths consider these adaptations unique to each individual. In accordance with this homeopathic principle, no two individuals will react to stressors in the same way, and neither will manifest exactly the same symptoms. This may be because we all have unique life experiences from which we learn different ways of coping with stress. Just as there are many shades of anger and many ways to display them, there are also a number of ways in which an individual may respond to, or display symptoms of, loss or bereavement. For each unique expression of an emotional state, there is a corresponding homeopathic remedy.[4]

When choosing a homeopathic remedy for any imbalance or disharmony, one looks at symptoms, either physical or emotional or both. Physical and emotional symptoms may be either objective or subjective. Objective symptoms are those that may be deduced simply by observation, such as "shivering in cold air" or "lameness upon rising." Subjective symptoms are those that are only known by the individual and are generally unknown by an observer, unless verbally expressed by the patient. Examples of subjective symptoms are "feeling chilly" and "experiencing panic attacks while in public places."

Some subjective symptoms that an animal may be experiencing simply cannot be known by observation. However, astute observation combined with logic can provide valuable clues to identifying some subjective symptoms in our animal companions.[5] In the case of "feeling chilly" we cannot be absolutely certain that Rover is feeling this way, but we may deduce so if we notice that he has a fondness for napping near (or even under!) the woodstove, on top of heating ducts, or in patches of sunlight on the floor, which he follows around the room with something resembling celestial regularity.

Similarly, we may not know for certain that Kitty experiences a panic attack each time she is taken into the waiting room of the veterinary clinic. But we may be reasonably certain that, since the meowing and scrabbling only occur after she has arrived at the clinic—and not while she is being placed in the transport carrier, or in the car, or on the way home, or in the privacy of her own backyard—that she is indeed experiencing some emotional response to being in a public place.

We can further deduce that Kitty is experiencing a panic attack rather than fear in general because of her degree of reaction. Simple fear in animals will usually take one of two forms. One is seen as shrinking, slinking, and slouching, with an avoidance of eye contact, in an effort to appear as small and unthreatening as possible to an assailant or foe. In the other, overt aggression is demonstrated: ears laid back and eyes shut to a slit (to protect them), teeth bared (to show potential power and danger), and body hair puffed out so as to appear as large and as formidable as possible to a real or imagined threat. In comparison, true panic lies several magnitudes above simple fear, and is characterized by violent, unfocused loss of control. This may take a variety of forms: lack of muscular coordination or control of bladder and bowel function or sometimes even limpness, as in the case of an animal so panic-stricken that it has simply given up all natural defense mechanisms. True panic may also be exhibited by violent, rageful behavior that continues long after a perceived threat to safety has been removed.

Remedies that are often indicated for severe panic include Aconitum, Gelsemium, Phosphorus, and Stramonium. To elucidate between them further, a study of each of these remedy's emotional (and sometimes, accompanying physical) symptoms is helpful.

The panic state of Aconitum is characterized by a suddenness of symptoms, being easily startled, and great restlessness and tossing about. Physical symptoms of Aconitum include shortness of breath that is loud, labored, and sometimes gasping and one foot that is cold while another is hot.

Gelsemium typifies classic stage fright: the subject is paralyzed with fear. Trembling and weak (or even limp) with fear, the Gelsemium subject may lose control of bladder or bowel, or muscular coordination. By degree, these symptoms resemble panic more than fear.

The panic state of Phosphorus is similar to that of Aconitum with a great tendency to jumpiness at the least noise or movement. But Phosphorus is far more timid than Aconitum, with an obvious vigilance or watchfulness, almost a dreaded expectation, that something will sneak out of a corner and attack. The Phosphorus cat or dog is the one who sheds copious amounts of fur in stressful situations.

Stramonium is the remedy best suited to the more violent displays of panic. This individual exhibits rapid and opposite emotional responses: at one moment he is seeking light and companionship, clinging almost fearfully to his caregiver, and in the next moment he will try violently to escape. The eye symptoms of Stramonium are singularly distinguishable; the eyes look too prominent, staring wide open, with pupils often dilated.

Not all emotional trauma occurs in our presence, however. For this reason, the importance of historical symptoms should not be overlooked. These symptoms stem from an incident in the past, sometimes one that occurred very long ago, but always leave both emotional and physical scars because the body holds the memory of everything that happens to it whether on an emotional or a physical level.[6] All emotional symptoms linger until they are healed (released), and if untreated, emotional symptoms will invariably evolve into physical symptoms.

The most common cases of an emotional historical symptom left untreated and causing a repetition of (unwarranted) emotional responses, and later, physical symptoms, is exemplified in many animals left in shelters. For the most part, especially those animals who had a reasonably good life with their former families, the experience of being left at a shelter is often interpreted as a form of loss or abandonment. Abandoned, forsaken, and suffering deep emotional trauma, these animals will often show an almost apathetic loss of trust and likely harbor a deep conviction that they are—at best—totally unlovable. They desperately want to be held, touched, and comforted, yet when such nurture is offered to them they pull back and withdraw. The hazard of trusting again and allowing themselves to feel loved is too great a risk, lest they experience again such deep betrayal and loss. They know on a very deep level that they cannot again survive such heartbreak without their very spirits breaking.

If they survive their abandonment and do not succumb to an in-house infection from a weakened immune system, and if they are lucky enough to be adopted, they are the cats and dogs who seem to have wrapped themselves in a protective layer of indifference, under which lurks deep insecurity. Once they are in a situation in which they feel safe, their layer of indifference falls away and they become so clingy, needy, and desperate for attention that they drive their people to distraction. On other occasions, they may totally resent and reject any and all attempts by their people to stroke, pet, or touch them. Sometimes, they vacillate unpredictably between behaviors, causing their people to begin to dislike them. They are the ones with varying, unaccountable digestive troubles, eating too quickly and vomiting or suffering from mysterious bouts of diarrhea for which the vet can determine no cause. Often they are the cats and dogs diagnosed with chronic "flea allergy dermatitis" (whether or not they have fleas). They may have itchy, scabby skin and wash, lick, and chew in an obsessive and compulsive manner. Unnurtured from without, they are no longer able to nurture themselves with nourishment from within, and as unloved and unlovable as they perceive themselves to be, they release their deep anguish and self-loathing through repetitive, compulsive self-mutilating behavior, much like human children who have been abused. The remedy, of course, is Natrum muriaticum, famous for resolving physical ailments brought on by deep emotional trauma.

After deciding which remedy to use for a particular emotional state, the next step is to choose the potency. As a general rule when using homeopathic remedies to help the body heal emotional states, the 200c potency is often used with great success.

In chronic, long-standing symptoms, one would use high potencies, say 200c to 1m. In cases of severe, acute symptoms, one would also use high potencies, say 30c to 200c, but only if sure of the remedy choice. If unsure, begin with a lower potency, perhaps 30c. It is unusual to use potencies higher than 200c, and often a wise choice to leave this kind of prescribing to a practitioner with many years of experience.[7]

One exception to the general rule is that the more recent an emotional symptom's origins, the lower the potency that may be used (12c to 30c) because the symptoms are still superficial within the psyche. Older or historic emotional symptoms often respond better to the higher potencies (30c to 200c) because by then they have become deeply embedded within the psyche and thus have become chronic.[8]

In all cases, an initial dose is given and allowed to do what healing it will, but it is not uncommon to give a second or even a third dose over the course of a few days or weeks. As always with homeopathic healing, doses are not repeated unless symptoms return, or begin to reassert themselves. This is even true if several months or years have passed since the last dose of a remedy.[9]

Acacia once fell down a set of circular stairs and had an interesting emotional response to the experience. She had been sitting on the sill of an octagonal window at the top of the stairs, when she slipped and fell away, the false window grating becoming tangled up in her legs. Fortunately, I arrived on the scene just as she was about to reach the bottom and caught her, which may have prevented actual sprains or broken bones. I immediately administered Bach Flower Calming Essence, for shock and fear, and followed that with several doses of Arnica 12c for bruising and trauma in general. The flower essence did much to relieve her fear and shock, but I noticed that she was still not herself.

It was several days before I was able to figure out that she was very angry about falling (what cat wouldn't be somewhat angry about falling and also have a deep sense of injured pride about the experience, or feel that her feline sense of grace and balance had somehow betrayed her?). Staphysagria ("anger with a deep sense of injustice," or even betrayal) resolved her lingering emotional symptoms. I used it in a 30c potency because it was a recent event. But had I not figured it out and treated her anger symptoms until six months had lapsed, I would have used Staphysagria 200c because it would then have become a historical symptom and chronic.

A list of emotional states with their specific manifestations and the homeopathic remedies that are useful in their resolution can be found in chapter 11. A materia medica of the remedies used for these specific emotional states is presented in chapter 12, and details both emotional and physical indications for each remedy. Flower essences and other herbal preparations may be useful in helping to resolve emotional states. Bach

Flower Calming Essence (also called Nature's Rescue) is also calming and soothing, especially during the initial phases of grief or if shock is an emotional component of the experience. Rescue Remedy was the original name given to the product by the first manufacturer, Ellon Bach (England). A New York company, Nelson Bach USA, bought out the patent from the parent company and renamed the product. Twice. The latest name, as of 1998, is "Nature's Rescue." Folks who've used the product for years still call it "Rescue Remedy," probably because the name rolls off the tongue more easily![10]

Another good formula for animal use is the herb and flower essence formula Broken Heart Remedy made by Avena Botanicals, which contains a combination of hawthorn flowers and berries, motherwort, lemon balm, heartsease pansy, and flower essences of hawthorn and heartsease pansy. Sources for this and other nonhomeopathic products can be found in appendix 4.

CHAPTER 9

Best Friends

Sunlight dappled the grass at my feet, shadows playing softly across the freshly dug hole. Sam sat near the edge hanging his head and sniffing at crumbs of the moist earth scattered in the grass. Occasionally, he would look at the cloth-wrapped bundle off to the side and up at me and then back at the hole.

Sam was a Norwegian forest cat and one of the most beautiful cats I'd ever seen. I'd known him since the moment of his birth, his mother having stayed at our farm long enough to leave us a magnificent litter of four, two of each gender. He'd had a difficult beginning, having to be nudged into the world bit by bit, as though he wasn't really sure he was ready. I remembered the sound of his first cry in the world, such a small sound, impatient with all the fuss and bother of being born. And now, he meowed again, but this time he was saying good-bye instead of hello.

We were burying Smudge, Sam's best friend in all the world; my other cat, black and white, timid as the wild thing he had been, born in the woods and given to me as his only chance for any kind of life. Smudge, who had taken his time looking me in the face, made me wait months before I could reach out and touch him without being bitten. A full year passed before I first picked him up and held him in my arms, and then he went limp from fright. All the moments of our small victories dammed up in my throat as I thought back on the morning of this day.

High summer was upon us, and both cats were out before breakfast, as usual. I'd gone out on the porch to call them to come in and eat. Sam was in the yard, but Smudge was oddly absent. When he didn't come after a moment, I gave it only a passing thought and went about the rest of the early morning chores. But the second I saw my neighbor walk into the yard, I somehow knew.

"Isn't that your cat, Patches?" she called out, using the wrong name as she passed the mailbox.

"Huh?" I said. "Where?" But I already knew without being told and was hurrying past her toward the road. Of course, it was another of those awful moments of my life. The dread built up in the back of my throat, hot, briny, and sharp as the scene quickly unfolded in my mind's eye.

He crossed blindly and without thinking when I called out, tail up, joyful expectation on his face, padding his way to a place where he felt safe, friends and food calling him home from his wanderings amid the rippling shadows that camouflaged mice and moles. But the remainder of the incident twisted and writhed in my intuitive second sight as the ghost sounds of tires and spewing gravel filled my ears. And then, inevitably, a huge, gaping hole centered itself around my heart, and I could no longer feel his living presence near me.

I grimly dug my heels into the incline that rose to the shoulder of the road, and likewise my fingernails found soft purchase in the palms of my hands. I found him lying on his side in the dusty gravel at the side of the road, as if in deep sleep. Strangely, there was not a mark on him, no outward appearance of injury. But as I reached out to pick him up, I sensed a deep and final stillness surrounding him. I knew he was gone, and I cursed my careless lack of attention in not ascertaining his exact whereabouts before calling him.

Now here I was facing another dark and gaping hole, the one that would cradle him until we met again on the other side of this corporeal plane. I gazed over at Sam, watching the light breeze rippling his brown and white tiger fur. He was looking down into the grave, his head hanging low over the edge. I spoke to him at that point, in as soothing and as calm a voice as I could muster, telling him of my sorrow in the part I had played in this tragedy and reminding him that Smudge was only a thought, a tug of the heart, away. Not surprisingly, he offered neither a glance nor a trill in reply.

Sam watched as I lowered Smudge gently into the hole and scooped in the coarse brown soil. A square of sod was remaindered from the beginning of the hole, and this I placed in the depression in the lawn. At this point, Sam got up, took several steps, and lay down on top of the grave. Resting his head on his paws, he closed his eyes and remained still. I sat awhile and gazed at him. This would be a difficult time for him, and I would need to be particularly attentive to his needs, both emotional and physical. I decided to let him stay there for a while to work out his grief in private, and getting up, I reached out to stroke his back between his shoulder blades. At this small touch, he flinched and drew away, and I knew that his grief had taken him to a place that not even I could soothe. Just how far his grief would take him would become evident to me in a matter of days.

Later that afternoon I stood on the porch watching him and calling him to dinner for a full ten minutes. He simply continued to lie there oblivious to my voice and my pleadings. Finally, I had to go out to the grave site and carry him into the house. As I scooped him into my arms, I could feel a tremendous heat rolling off his body in waves, not a natural heat but one of a high fever. As I expected, he refused to eat and went into the living room and lay in a cool corner away from the evening activity of the family.

Still later, as I was washing up the dinner dishes, I heard a series of explosive sneezes coming from the direction of the living room. Turning the corner, I saw Sam shake his head, run his tongue over his nose and swipe at his face with one paw. Although I knew that he was fully vaccinated for every possible contagion, and no reports of feline upper respiratory virus had reached my ears, a warning buzzed just below my consciousness. Uh oh, I thought, this does not look good.

His fever and bouts of sneezing continued to escalate over the course of the evening and night. By three in the morning both eyes were streaming with a watery discharge, and he was shivering with chills. In all my years of working at animal shelters, I had never seen such a rapidly developing case of upper respiratory virus in a cat. I fetched an electric blanket and made a cozy nest around him. Pulling out all the stops, I tried to entice him to eat, tempting him with all his favorite treats: smashed sardines in olive oil, mackerel, slices of roast beef from the deli, shaved turkey breast, smoked trout. He would touch nothing, refusing even to lick off the morsels I smeared across his mouth.

With the approach of dawn, I began to see how weak he was rapidly becoming, and I realized he had not used his cat box to urinate or even moved. I began giving him water with an eyedropper, counting off thirty-minute blocks of time until the veterinary clinic staff would come on duty.

At nine that morning I called the clinic. The vet recommended the usual round of standard antibiotics and antihistamines, and I took a precious hour to go and pick them up. But by noon, after the recommended dose of each, I saw that he was worsening, eyes and nose crusting up with a thick, white discharge, even though his fever had decreased to just two degrees above normal. These symptoms I knew were indicative of the second stage of the virus; the fever had receded a bit—an indication that the body was mounting less of an attack against the invading pathogen—and destroyed cells were evident in great numbers in the colored discharges that were now appearing. Although I knew that the antibiotics were of no help, I kept using them because, at the time, I had not learned about homeopathy, and conventional medicine was all I had in my repertoire.

By the second evening of his illness Sam was not only weaker, but he refused water and all forms of comfort. He would turn his head away from even the smallest gesture of help I offered, and my spirits sank as hope dwindled. At ten that evening, I removed the electric blanket and made a tent over him with a thick quilt. I built a warm fire in the woodstove, even though the night air was a summery seventy degrees, and brought out the humidifier to see if warm, moist air would relieve his breathing difficulties.

For the next few hours he lay in his humid tent, placidly and limply, with only an occasional rasping gasp to indicate that he was still with me. Again, I marked off blocks of time with water drops from an eyedropper placed on the edge of his lips. As with any small gesture of comfort, he shrugged off this small nourishment, letting the drops roll down the side of his chin and onto his paws, where I wiped them away with a soft cloth. I knew we were losing ground—and rapidly, too.

In exhaustion, I fell asleep beside him and woke several hours before dawn. As soon as I reached out to touch him I knew he was gone, having receded from the physical world shortly after I had fallen asleep. I wondered if perhaps he had chosen that moment to leave because my attention was elsewhere, and I was no longer keeping him with me by sheer force of will. And at that thought a fleeting recognition occurred: I was so focused on desperately trying to avoid a second loss in as many days that I had not seen his true illness—a broken heart.

In retrospect, had I known about the wonderful efficacy of homeopathic remedies at the time, Ignatia would have been the first remedy I would have given him. Although the respiratory symptoms of Ignatia lean more toward dry, spasmodic coughs, it was a remedy that fit his emotional state, as Dr. Boericke describes in his *Pocket Manual of Homoeopathic Materia Medica:* "Introspective; silently brooding, melancholic, sad, tearful; not communicating; after shocks, grief and disappointment."[1] It was certainly true that Sam's physical symptoms were immediately preceded by his emotional state, and I have since learned the validity of Dr. Edward Bach's insight that all symptoms of physical disease begin in the emotional sphere.

If Ignatia had not entirely healed Sam's emotional state and his physical symptoms escalated to wet, watery sneezing, I would have pushed forward to the use of Natrum muriaticum 30c, as the symptom picture of that remedy fit his initial upper respiratory symptoms exactly. As Dr. Boericke describes the respiratory symptoms in his monograph on Nat mur: "Violent, fluent coryza (e. g., head cold), changing to stoppage of nose, making breathing difficult. Discharge thin and watery, like raw white of egg. Violent sneezing coryza. Infallible for stopping a cold commencing with sneezing. Use thirtieth potency. Loss of smell and taste."[2]

Possibly more importantly, because the mental and emotional symptoms of an individual are the symptoms of most significance, Nat mur would have addressed Sam's mental state, which matched Dr. Boericke's indication for the remedy, "Psychic causes of disease; ill effects of grief, fright, anger, etc."[3]

Decades later, Acacia, whom many of you may know from other homeopathic healing stories I've recounted, rebounded strongly and rapidly from feline upper respiratory virus by the application of Natrum muriaticum 30c. The newest antibiotic therapy had no effect on her response to the course of the illness, largely because it was a viral infection, for which antibiotics are useless. But three days of doses of Natrum muriaticum 30c—a single dose each time her sneezing and watery eye symptoms returned—proved heroic from the very first dose. With each dose she slept deeply and woke refreshed, hungry, and feeling well enough to interact with those around her. How I wish I had known all this when Sam was with me, but life is a process of discovery and claiming understanding and its power for our own.

We may ask ourselves whether or not it is possible for animals to grieve at a loss, or even to experience and express emotions. My experience with Sam opened my eyes to a whole new dimension—the reality that animals may experience emotions in much the same ways as we do. The fact is, I had never seen and still have never seen upper respiratory virus claim a cat in two days. What I can only surmise is that his emotional state made his immune system extremely vulnerable, and he lost his will to live, despite my efforts and my reluctance to let him go.

He rests now beside his beloved friend. In my mind's eye, I see them together, chasing shadows and each other through the underbrush of the woods. One day I'll find them there. One day, when we're all called home.

CHAPTER 10

Moving Onward

There inevitably comes a time in our process of saying good-bye to someone we love when everything that needs to be done has been done. We've met, nurtured, and grown to love our animal friend. We've had what life together we were blessed to have. This time may have been long, and we may have had the unique gift of watching our friend mature and become elderly.

For some of us, the last days, weeks, or months with our animal companions may have been spent attending to their needs as illness or mishap took them from us. Some of us have had to make the difficult decision to choose euthanasia, while others of us have experienced our companion's natural death process. Usually, the experiences we have been through have been shared with other members of our families, human and animal alike. Through sharing our experiences with our surviving animal family members, we have learned that grief is not a process reserved exclusively for the humans and is as much a part of life as the transition we call dying.

Throughout our long journey we have experienced our grief in its myriad components and forms, sometimes surprising or even shocking but always fully realized. Some of us have processed our grief in a single year's time, but grief lasting years is not uncommon among humans or animals.

The act of burial or cremation and memorial has served as a period of transition in our process of grief. We all hope that these physical rituals will somehow contain the emotional trauma of our loss, shut a door, complete the final chapter of a life we were privileged to share. Afterward, when the duties and ceremonies of our memorial day are done, we may notice with dismay that our pain is still very present and fresh. Slowly we come to understand that there is more to the journey of loss than the final, physical act of saying good-bye.

Various descriptive names have been given to the final stages of grief and healing from loss: acceptance, resolution, moving onward. For most of us, acceptance does not always mean that we have graduated and finished with our feelings of loss. Surrender to the reality of loss does not mean that we do not deeply long for "just one more hug." For many of us memories remain bittersweet, and sometimes these vignettes catch us unaware in surprising places and unguarded moments. The particular slant of late-day light can transport us back to our companion's final moments, or we may briefly glimpse in a passing car an adolescent puppy waving the plume of his tail in the back window in exactly the same way as our Sparky. Our tears of loss and feelings of separation well up anew. And while feelings of loss may resurface months or years after we have said our final good-byes, for many of us it is difficult to give ourselves permission to grieve as deeply or as fiercely as we have loved. Still, it is important to try to work through our grief. Our feelings, even feelings that may be uncomfortable, are evidence that we are in a process of healing. And it is vital for us to remember that we are involved in the *process* of living, that life is never an unmoving event.

What remains for us to do now is to claim our new lives. We are changed, stronger and very different people than when we began our journey. We have undergone an experience that has cast light on the deepest parts of our humanity. We've grown to understand that we can experience a relationship from beginning to end. We can undertake the responsibilities inherent in that relationship in such a way that we feel good about ourselves, our actions, and our choices. We have learned the timeless arts of self-acceptance and self-forgiveness. In loving our animal companion, we may even have learned to love ourselves. Perhaps we have experienced feelings of inadequacy at not being able to save our animal companion from death. But even in this, many of us will come to the understanding that dying is the last act of living, and if we were present with our animal companion in this, then we can take great comfort in knowing that we were fully present for him or her in all things. Others of us may have relived having to make difficult decisions and choices, but most of us come to understand that choices made out of true love are never wrong choices.

None of this means that we no longer miss our beloved friend or have no more feelings to work through: it simply means that we are now ready to take another step on our journey of healing from loss. New schedules without our cherished animal companions may at first seem uncomfortable. Filling these voids of time or even empty places in our homes may take a bit of practice and self-exploration, but time itself is a great healer. It is very important that the voids be filled naturally, as we become ready to fill them. Just as it was good to practice self-care during the earlier stages of our grieving, we now have another occasion to care for ourselves with the same tenderness with which we tended our animal companion's needs. Good self-care during this phase of our healing means easing ourselves into new activities. We must remember not to rush headlong into new things in an unconscious attempt to escape lingering feelings of loss and grief.

We will know that we are ready to undertake new things when new things come naturally to us. That first morning will come when we do not automatically reach for our animal companion's food bowl or add to our grocery list items for making our friend's favorite treat. Very likely that first time will be a surprise, and we will wonder to ourselves what we should be doing instead. But as the occasions occur again and again, we will find ourselves doing other things in their place: having our breakfast on the sunny deck or rearranging our morning schedule. We will not be forgetting our companion, but we will be resuming our daily rituals of life.

Some of us may find that we have surviving animal companions still at home with us. Good care for them is vital to their recovery from loss, too. Like humans, animals need to ease themselves into new situations. They, too, will find that their daily schedules have changed, and they will be able to adjust more readily if we can provide them with reassurance and comfort when they indicate their need for emotional support. In all things we simply need to do the best we can do, but this does not mean that we need strive for perfection. It is not uncommon for many of us to shy away from remaining animal companions out of lingering sorrow or even fear that we cannot meet their emotional needs. Some of us may have experienced our loss so deeply that we feel emotionally bankrupt, and even the thought of interacting with our other animal companions leaves us feeling further drained. We are not bad people if we cannot meet our remaining animal companion's needs for emotional support during this stage of our healing from loss. We can recognize our human limitations and practice good self-care for everyone involved. We can give ourselves permission to ask others in our lives to spend quality time with these animal companions. We can hire a dog- or cat-sitter to spend time with our animal companion when we are at work or ask a neighbor to take him or her to the groomer or out for a walk or romp in the park. Sometimes, when we have had some respite from having to be emotionally involved with our other animal family members so soon after a loss, we find that our interactions with these other animal family members will come naturally once again.

A time may come when we begin to think of welcoming another animal companion into our homes and lives. This may be for our own needs alone or to provide companionship for a remaining animal that has lost a buddy. For some of us, feelings of confusion and guilt may arise: are we betraying the memory of our cherished animal companion by replacing him or her with another?[1] Needing love and companionship in our lives has nothing to do with the animal companions we have said good-bye to or have lived with in the past. It is important to remember that the choice to adopt another animal companion will also come naturally to us if we have given ourselves ample time to experience feelings of loss.

For our surviving animal family members, opening the family pack or pride structure to a new member may not be easy. As we have learned, the social structures of animal groups are very complicated, and their establishment takes time and reorganization. Introducing a new animal into the family gradually is a good way to include animal companions in the selection process.

Many people have found that introducing their animal companion to a potential newcomer in a neutral territory, such as a side yard or public park, is a good way for everyone to get acquainted. A few such meetings, not lasting more than fifteen minutes, will often have very telling results: either the animals will establish a rapport or they won't. Later, the newcomer may be less likely to cause dissension when brought to your home for further "let's get acquainted" sessions.

For those people who have cats, public places may not be the ideal place to get acquainted. Many people who live with cats find that a small room in the house, one closed off from other areas, makes a useful meeting place for felines. When introducing animals to one another, never leave them unsupervised. As ambassadors for our animal companions, we must at all times be ready to protect them and oversee their safety and well-being. This is also true for the newcomer; he or she will be in a new and perhaps threatening situation, and we, as their stewards, must look out for their well-being, too.

Like humans, animals also experience loneliness. Having a new friend to play with may be just the thing that a solitary animal needs, especially if she has become accustomed to spending the day playing with another of her kind when all the human family members are away at work. In addition, animals who have grieved deeply over the loss of a playmate may benefit from a change in daily activities; developing and sustaining new relationships is as much a part of their healing process from loss as it is ours.

Sometimes a surviving animal companion will enthusiastically welcome a new addition into the family. This is especially true if the new member is younger or smaller than our resident animal companion. The reason for this lies in the pecking order of the pack and pride hierarchy. Younger, smaller animals are less threatening (and easier to establish rank with) than older, larger animals. Animal hierarchy within any pack or pride will usually sort itself out if we are patient and attentive to the emotional needs of the animals involved.

When introducing a new animal into the family, it is a good idea to always support the emotional needs of the resident animal. This is especially true of cats. In extreme situations many people have found that open displays of affection toward their resident cat, in full view of a newcomer, is not only deeply reassuring to him or her, but also sends a strong nonverbal message to the newcomer: "you're a newcomer, and you will not usurp this other cat's place in the existing order of our pride." Such open displays of affection assist our resident cat in establishing "ownership" of the humans within the pride, and most new cats, seeing boundaries firmly set by the food provider of the pride (people) will quickly comply with the existing pecking order.

When bringing Cat into our family, I made a very serious mistake in my relationship with Acacia because I did not follow this protocol. Fortunately, the situation was quickly resolved because I recognized my error and corrected it. While I was giving Acacia needed attention, I also had some misgivings about how Cat would react to being shut off from interactions with me, because of her recent emotional trauma and her extraordinary need for reassurance. But I needn't have worried; Cat was distracted with exploring her new territory without interference, and she accepted my behavior as "normal cat behavior," because this is how cats normally interact within the pride.

This is also true of dogs within the grouping of the pack. Both species will initially approach a newcomer, sniff, and have a brief interaction— sometimes benign, other times more physically boisterous. The newcomer will then be ignored for a time, until he or she begins to test the boundaries of rank and file. What follows is a reorganization of the pack or pride structure. To humans, this period of restructuring may look or seem like total chaos; we may think that there will never again be a moment of peace in our house. But rest assured, things will calm down, and the new social structure will assert itself. Everyone will find his or her rightful place based on age, gender, physical prowess, and the intricate nuances of species-specific rules of hierarchy.

This occurs when a new animal comes to reside with a single animal resident as well as when one or more animals enter or leave an existing animal group. A friend of mine shared her home with ten cats that she had adopted over a long period of time. One autumn two of her cats disappeared, likely the result of a hunting fisher or bobcat. Although the remaining cats had lived together for a very long time, anarchy broke out among the ranks three weeks after the two disappeared. Everyone scrambled to assert a new position in the remaming pride; two vacancies left more than two slots—a ripple went through the whole pride and the entire group needed to be restructured.

Fighting, open displays of aggression and antagonism, and bids for superiority over food bowls and litter boxes ensued between the remaining cats in this household. Not always small spats, these tiffs sometimes became vicious brawls and occurred not only between cats who had a passing acquaintance with each other but also between cats who had shared sleeping places and washed one another's whiskers. New alliances were formed; new sleeping partners and playmates were tried out, discarded, and replaced. With each new adjustment a new wave of interactions occurred down through the ranks. Finally, after three months, everyone seemed to find an acceptable place and rank, and things calmed down, with only an occasional rumble when someone forgot his or her new placement in the sequence of the pride.

In households where a newcomer and resident cat are the only animals, there can also be a shifting in pride status. Because of this and her recent loss of McTavish, I had another concern about how Acacia would interpret Cat's arrival. I remembered that when McTavish became ill and subsequently died, Acacia then gained first-cat position. I was very worried that she would emotionally or mentally interpret the sequence of events as a pattern that would be repeated. I wondered if she expected that Cat's arrival also meant that she, too, would become ill and defer first-cat place to another newcomer. This was an especially disconcerting thought when she became ill with another relapse of her formerly chronic complaints.

Looking back on the situation, I now doubt that Acacia interpreted events in exactly this manner, and I have since learned a valuable lesson from my animal communicator friend: human definitions don't necessarily apply to animal behavior. I do think, though, that Acacia's abandonment issues surfaced with my mishandling of the situation. I also suspect that her delicate constitutional state was weakened by the arrival of another cat in our home. But fortunately, correcting my behavior and using her constitutional remedy resolved the problem.

Although it took such a lesson to reinforce the rules I know I should follow, in this too, I have been willing to exercise self-forgiveness. Consequently, I made a firm promise to myself to not repeat the same mistake again but gave myself permission to be fully human and imperfect at times. It is imperfection that we as humans are very good at. We must make mistakes in order to learn that we have options of doing things a different way.

In our journeys with our animal friends, we have learned many things about them, the world around us, and even new things about ourselves. It may be that the purest form of love that our animal companions extend to us is to walk by our side on our voyage back to ourselves. As we are their corporeal stewards during their time here on earth, perhaps they are our spiritual stewards. Love is a symbiotic alliance. The timeless saying holds true for both participants in such a union: the heart that is loved never forgets.

CHAPTER 11

A Homeopathic Repertory of Specific Emotional States

ANGER

WITH:	REMEDY
Aggression (biting)	Bell, Nux v
Growling or grumbling	Bell, Nux v
Impatience:	
in general	Caps, Cina, Croc, Nux v, Sep
better with consolation	Puls
worse with consolation	Cham
Jealousy	Apis, Lach, Staph
Sense of injustice	Staph
Pacing	Ars, Rhus t
Possessiveness or territorial	Bell, Nux v
Resentment	Staph
Restlessness:	
in general	Acon, Ars, Cham, Coff, Ign, Rhus t, Stram
morning on rising	Rhus t
at night	Ars

RAGE

WITH:	REMEDY
Rage in general	Bell, Hyos, Stram
From:	
being left alone/behind	Hyos, Ph ac, Stram
being touched	Bell, Stram
having collar around the neck	Lach, Staph
having the throat touched	Canth, Lach, Staph
Simmering	Cham, Staph
Violent	Stram
enough to kill	Hyos, Lyss, Plat, Stram
explosive, but short-lived	Bell, Hep, Hyos, Merc
With:	
fright	Acon, Aur, Bell, Calc
panic	Acon, Gels, Phos, Stram

SADNESS AND GRIEF

WITH:	REMEDY
Distress at being looked at	Ars
Deep bereavement:	
apathy (indifference)	Carb v, Nat m, Nat p, Ph ac
sighing	Ign
Depression, sleeps from sadness	Nat m
From:	
abandonment	Aur, Bor, Ign, Lach, Nat m, Puls
despair about others	Aur
longing	Nat m, Sil
loneliness (abandoned)	Aur, Psor, Puls, Nat m
Loss of:	
former family	Ign, Nat m
home	Caps, Carb an, Ph ac

SADNESS AND GRIEF (CONTINUED)

WITH:	REMEDY
Loss of: *(continued)*	
loved one/offspring	Ign, Nat m
trust (general)	Ign, Nat m, Puls, Sil, Sulph
trust (in young and elderly)	Bar c
Sadness, constant and chronic	Graph
Searches for one gone	Aur, Ign, Nat m
Silent grief	Ign, Nat m, Ph ac

FEAR

OF:	REMEDY
being alone	Caps, Hyos, Ign, Kali c, Lyc, Ph ac, Phos, Puls, Stram
being touched	Arn, Cham (strikes out when touched), Lach (throat), Nux
bright lights (shuns light)	Con
children	Bar c, Lyc
downward motion	Bor
falling	Bor, Cupr, Gels, Lac c, Lil t
riding in a car	Bell
scolding	Bell, Nat m, Plat, Staph
strangers	Hyos, Lyc, Nat c, Rhus t
thunderstorms	Nat c, Nat m, Nit ac, Phos, Rhod, Sep

WITH:	REMEDY
Anxiety or apprehension	Arg n, Gels
Barking and howling	Apis, Camph, Cic, Cupr, Kali c, Lyc, Plat, Stram, Verat
at night	Verat
before urinating	Bor, Lyc
during thunderstorm	Gels
Severe panic	Acon, Gels, Phos, Stram
Stubbornness	Sil, Sulph
Timidity	Bar c, Bor, Ign, Nat m, Puls, Sil, Sulph

DESIRES AND AVERSIONS

(Not pure emotional states but peculiar, and may lead to the selection of a helpful remedy.)

DESIRES:	REMEDY
Cool air	Sulph
Company	Coff, Gels, Nat m, Stram
Darkness	Lyss
Heat/warmth	Nat m, Psor
Things,	
but doesn't know what	Bry
Things,	
but rejects them	Cham
To:	
hide (in closets, etc.)	Bell, Hell, Lyss, Nit ac, Phos, Puls, Stram
hide (from youngsters	
and elders)	Bar c
To be:	
carried (only)	Nat m, Puls
carried, but bites	Cham
carried/rocked/caressed	Puls
off somewhere all the time	
(to roam, wander)	Lach

AVERSIONS TO:	REMEDY
being carried	Cham
company	Lyc, Lyss, Sil
consolation	Cham, Nat m
the dark	Ars, Phos, Stram
heat	Sulph
noise	Phos
offspring	Lac c
open spaces	Bor, Ph ac
public places	Am c, Gels
water	Lyss

CHAPTER 12

A Materia Medica of Common Homeopathic Remedies

Aconitum napellus (Monkshood)

Great fear, worry, anxiety, and anguish characterize every ailment, both emotional and physical. Easily startled. All pains and symptoms intolerable. Does not want to be touched. Sudden and great sinking of strength. Complaints that come on suddenly from exposure to cold, dry winds, or very hot weather (especially digestive symptoms). Aconite individuals feel better in open air and their symptoms are worse in a warm room, at night, and from cold, dry winds.

Ammonium carbonicum (Carbonate of Ammonia)

This remedy presents a difficult individual: bad-tempered and gloomy, especially in bad weather, made worse by interactions with others (does not want to be spoken to); sad, weepy, and difficult; and does not like to keep him- or herself clean. The general physical appearance of this remedy type is a slow-reacting, heavy, and sedentary individual who is always tired and overworked and greatly sensitive to cold air; these individuals are prone to respiratory symptoms and have an extreme dislike for water, either for drinking or bathing, and often have a very strong acidlike body odor from uncleanliness. Symptoms become worse when the individual falls asleep, with motion, and from all forms of cold, including cold weather, damp days, cloudy days, getting the body cold, and in raw, open air. Symptoms are relieved by pressure, eating, and lying on the abdomen.

Apis mellifica (Honeybee)

Emotional symptoms include apathy or indifference, or visible stupor alternating with frenzied behavior; these individuals are listless and fidgety, displaying a general anxiousness associated with their symptoms, and have emotional symptoms that change, often with great rapidity: jealousy, fearfulness, rage, or grief; they are awkward in their movements (stumbling or spilling things) and can be whining and hard to please. General guiding physical symptoms relate to those caused by a bee sting: swelling and edema or puffing up of various parts, intolerance of heat, general soreness, great sensitivity to the slightest touch, and afternoon aggravation of symptoms. All forms of heat make the symptoms worse: warm rooms, hot weather, the warmth of a fireplace, too warm a bed, and hot baths. Symptoms are also made worse by touch (even touching the hair), after sleeping, from any pressure, and also daily at four in the afternoon. Relief of symptoms occurs in open air, when uncovered, and during cold bathing.

Argentum nitricum (Nitrate of Silver)

These are very fearful and nervous individuals with a tendency to tremors and faintness. They are depressed with a weak memory and often very impulsive, wanting to do things in a hurry. All fears, anxieties, and emotional reactions of Argentum individuals are fueled by unwarranted impulses and hastiness. Even diarrhea originates from fear. Of the physical symptoms, the brain, spinal nerves, and mucous membranes of these individuals all show symptoms. The individual seems mentally tired and worn out and experiences physical debility and trembling. Symptoms of the spinal nerves appear in the legs with trembling, debility, rigidity of the calves, walking and standing unsteadily, and numbness of the forelegs. Mucous membranes are inflamed; conjunctivitis of the eyes (red, swollen, ulcerations with thick, abundant, yellow discharges) is a common symptom; the nose runs and itches and there is much sneezing; respiratory symptoms include hoarseness and a heavy cough, as though there is a hair stuck in the throat. Physical symptoms are made worse when the individual becomes anxious or hesitant; from sweets; in closed, stuffy rooms; looking down; when drinking; and in a crowd (they feel as though they cannot breathe). Cool, open air, as well as bathing in cool water, hard pressure, and motion all bring relief.

Arnica montana (Leopard's Bane)

Although usually associated with physical symptoms that result from falls, blows, and contusions, Arnica has distinctive emotional symptoms. These individuals are very fearful of being approached or touched, very nervous, and unable to bear pain. All sensations are magnified to an unbearable degree, and individuals may seem indifferent to company or consolation, or even morose or delirious, simply because they want to be left alone. They are extremely fearful of open or large spaces. Arnica is a good remedy to consider after shock. Physically, these individuals are sore, bruised, and restless but mentally exhausted or even apathetic. Symptoms are made worse from work, being jostled, and after shocks, bruises, and sprains. Relief comes from lying with the head low or lying stretched out.

Arsenicum album (Arsenic Trioxide)

A great remedy, especially when anxiety is precipitated by anger. These individuals trust only important people or significant people and are preoccupied with cleanliness or fastidiousness. They exhibit great anxiety and restlessness with a need to change place constantly; they are extremely fearful of being left alone, yet resist attention, especially when being given a remedy. They are despairing, malicious, and selfish, yet lack courage. General symptoms of the Arsenicum individual are characterized by debility, exhaustion (after the slightest effort), and restlessness, with nightly aggravation of symptoms. Arsenicum symptoms are generally worse after cold drinks, food, and air, and from eating vegetables (which aggravates the diarrhea). Hot things, such as hot, dry compresses, hot food and drinks, all bring relief of symptoms. Symptoms are also improved by walking or moving around, elevating the head, sitting straight up, and company.

Aurum metallicum (Metallic Gold)

This remedy is well suited to those individuals who suffer from profound despondency with a sense of utter worthlessness and self-condemnation. They are easily irritated and fierce at the slightest contradiction; do not like company or companionship; and cannot do things fast enough. Characteristically, they are hopeless, despondent, and depressed, with a loss of joy about life and living. They prefer solitude and are extremely sensitive to noise, confusion, and excitement. Physically, the vascular system, bones, and glands all show symptoms. Heart and circulatory symptoms include a rapid, feeble, and irregular pulse and high blood pressure. The bones seem to self-destruct; pain in the bones of the head with lumps under the scalp; degeneration of the bones of the nose, palate, and mastoid bone (the protruding bone behind the ear). Symptoms are made worse from mental work, cold, and during the night (from sunset to sunrise). Cool, open air; bathing in cold water; becoming warm; and walking all bring relief.

Baryta carbonica (Carbonate of Baryta)

Baryta is especially suited to the very young and the very old. Shy and timid, these individuals exhibit a distinct lack of self-confidence. They may seem forgetful and confused, which may result in an aversion to strangers or even childishness. They seem to be particularly bothered by small, insignificant things or events. Physically, these individuals will seem weak, weary, and extremely sensitive to cold; they often must sit, lie down, or lean on something. Baryta symptoms are always relieved when walking outdoors. This remedy is slow in action and bears repetition well.

Belladonna (Deadly Nightshade)

If anger is so volatile as to be expressed as rage—especially if the eyes are glassy and the pupils are chronically dilated—Belladonna is well indicated. Belladonna individuals will typically be unpredictable in interactions with others; one never knows when they will strike out or bite; one moment they are happy and gregarious, the next hissing, growling, or lashing out. The Belladonna cat or dog grumbles and growls at no one or nothing in particular. Symptoms are made worse from the heat of the sun or getting too warm; from cold drafts of air on the head; light, noise, or jarring; company; touch and pressure; and motion. Bending backward and resting relieve symptoms.

Borax (Borate of Sodium)

Excessively nervous and easily frightened, Borax individuals may have had an emotional trauma that resulted in their particular emotional state. These individuals have a very peculiar nervous symptom: an extreme dread of all downward motion. They exhibit terror at any movement that causes their body to move in a downward direction: rocking, being carried downstairs, being put down, or being laid down. In this, their terror is so great that their face will assume an anxious expression, and they will thrust out the forelimbs as if terrified of falling. They exhibit an extreme sensitivity to sudden noises: the blast of a firearm, thunder, and other loud, sudden noises will cause a reaction of violent fear.

Physically, Borax symptoms include gastrointestinal complaints of salivation, nausea, vomiting, colic, and diarrhea as well as skin eruptions wherein slight injuries become easily inflamed. Interestingly, these individuals may have hair or fur that tangles easily at the ends. Borax symptoms are always worse with downward motion, from noise, and in warm weather; they are better from pressure, in the evening, and during cold weather.

Bryonia (Wild Hops)

Bryonia individuals display irritability when pressured by others or by external events; they exhibit a grouchiness that escalates into anxiety and finally, rage; they are quick to become angry, and symptoms of anger are relieved by purging, that is, vomiting, moving the bowels, or emotional outbursts. Soothing or consolation does not relieve their anger. They are very shy with strangers but are violently eruptive with familiars. Their symptoms are worse with downward motion, when exposed to sudden noises, during cold, from getting wet, and after eating fruit. They are better only during a certain time of day: eleven at night.

Calcarea carbonica (Carbonate of Lime)

Apprehensive and definitely worse toward evening, Calcarea types are fearful of pending losses. They may seem forgetful or confused, low-spirited, and anxious—even obstinate. They are adverse to work or mental exertion and will often want to be held in a lap as long as they are not bothered. They must have attention, but only with a minimum of effort on their part and only on their own terms. Often described as fair, fat, flabby, damp, perspiring, and sour, Calcarea individuals grew either too quickly or too slowly in youth. They often have big heads, big abdomens, and ravenous appetites.

Because impaired nutrition is within the sphere of this remedy, these individuals will often have physical symptoms involving the glands, skin, and bones. They take cold easily, being overly sensitive to it; crave eggs; and eat undigestible things such as dirt, lime, or chalk; and are prone to diarrhea. Their skin seems malnourished and unhealthy: pale and loose with a loss of elasticity. Bone development is often hampered: they've either grown too quickly resulting in big bones with no real substance or strength, or the bones have grown too slowly from an imperfection in the body's ability to absorb and utilize calcium, phosphorus, and vitamin D; in either case their limbs are weak, especially the knees, and they may have difficulty walking. Symptoms are worse from any form of cold, work, or exertion and worse at the teething stage of puppies or during adolescent puberty. No situations or applications bring relief of symptoms.

Camphora (Camphor)

This is one the remedies to consider in states of sudden collapse resulting from fright or emotional trauma. After a sudden sinking of strength, the whole body is icy cold (even the tongue, which may also tremble) and body temperature and pulse are subnormal. It is very characteristic of Camphor individuals that despite the icy coldness of their body, they refuse to be covered or warmed, and although collapsed, may exhibit extreme restlessness. The upper lip is pulled back, there is a burning thirst, the voice is hoarse, and the breath is cold. All symptoms are worse from mental exertion, shock, and cold drafts. This is a remedy used in cases of heatstroke when the body is so overheated and dried that even the sweat glands lose function. Therefore, symptoms improve when sweat is restored and with the appearance of discharges.

Cantharis (Spanish Fly)

Violent inflammations and extreme oversensitiveness characterize this remedy state both emotionally and physically. Furious delirium and anxious restlessness end in rage and violent, frenzied behavior. These individuals constantly attempt to do something but achieve nothing. The emotional state quickly escalates into acute fury, sometimes of a sexual nature. Acute physical symptoms of this remedy include violent inflammation of the gastrointestinal tract, especially the lower bowel; the urinary and sexual organs are likewise affected. There is a disgust for all foods and especially for drinks even though there may be a burning thirst. All symptoms are worse from light touch (especially around the throat), being approached, and drinking fluids; and better from rubbing or massage.

Capsicum (Cayenne Pepper)

Like the herb, Capsicum individuals have a peppery mental disposition. Excessively ill-tempered, they simply want to be left alone and are often seemingly homesick and sleepless. However, their spicy state does not extend to their physical symptoms. Rather, they are seen to be weak and limp, with a lack of body heat and little reactive physical force. Many are also fat, dislike physical exertion, and disinclined to alter their daily routines. They exemplify a physical state of exhausted vitality from overexertion because of poor living habits or mental strain, other times from simple overwork or being overwrought, and in this too, they have little physical power to recuperate. Capsicum individuals are much like Sulphur individuals in their lack of desire to bathe or be bathed. They are always thirsty, but drinking causes them to tremble. Capsicum symptoms are worse from open air, being uncovered, and in cold air and better while eating and from all forms of heat.

Carbo animalis (Animal Charcoal)

With a great desire to be left alone, Carbo animalis individuals do not want any company and seem very sad. Their sadness transforms into anxiety with the coming night. But come morning, they are once again depressed and thoughtful. This is a remedy that is especially well suited for older individuals who have experienced exhausting situations, both great emotional strain and physical illness, which leave them with weak blood circulation and lowered physical vitality. Often we will note that their hearing is somehow impaired, for they seem unable to tell the direction from which sounds are coming. Their symptoms are worse from any intervention, and nothing relieves them.

Carbo vegetabilis (Vegetable Charcoal)

Mentally, these individuals are fearful of the dark and need light and companionship. They may stare and seem frightened, as though seeing a ghost. In this, their fears seem to be caused by things only they can see. Physically, typical Carbo vegetabilis individuals are fat, sluggish, and lazy, and their complaints tend to be chronic. Their bodies are cold and lifeless, but their heads are hot. Frequently their lowered physical functions manifest as feeble pulse, rapid breathing, and weakness; they must have fresh air, be fanned, or have the windows open. All Carbo vegetabilis symptoms are worse at night and in the evening and from cold, from fatty food, or from warm, damp weather. Symptoms are relieved by cool air and elevating the feet.

Chamomilla (German Chamomile)

These individuals are spiteful and snappish, impulsive, and vehement; quick as a storm; irritated by very small things; possess impatience without ambition; and do not want help. They are often kickers and biters and cannot control their anger or impulses; they exhibit anger with restlessness that is alleviated by quick motions. Symptoms are worse around nine in the evening, in cold, damp air, and in the wind. Being carried, mild weather, heat, sweating, and cold compresses relieve symptoms.

Cicuta virosa (Water Hemlock)

The mental state of Cicuta is most peculiar. Gloomy and grieving, yet strangely indifferent to their surroundings, Cicuta individuals seem to be in a world of their own. They may be mistrustful or suffer from convulsive behavior, bending the head, neck, and spine far backward in violent contortions. With or without these odd bodily distortions, these individuals often moan and whine while awake or while dreaming, and severe emotional trauma may lie at the root of these strange behaviors. As with Calcarea carbonica types, there is a desire to eat unusual things, such as coal. Great thirst is relieved by drinking but followed by hiccups. There is nothing that makes Cicuta symptoms better, while touch, drinks, and movement of the head make all symptoms worse.

Cina (Worm Seed)

Cina is appropriate for individuals who are nervous and irritable. Cross, cranky, temperamental, and disagreeable, Cina individuals display an aversion to being touched, bothered in any way, or carried. It is difficult to please them; they will ask for many things, but reject everything offered, and in this, they are very much like Chamomilla. Physically, they are very hungry, especially in the morning after waking and just before mealtimes, but will experience vomiting and diarrhea immediately after eating or drinking. They are also prone to various twitching and trembling movements: violent jerking of the feet, especially the hind feet, which are stretched out spasmodically. All symptoms are worse from staring at objects, at night, in the sun, and in summer. Symptoms are improved with motion.

Coffea cruda (Unroasted Coffee)

Coffea is useful for symptoms caused by the ill effects of sudden emotions and shocks. Coffea is appropriate for individuals who suffer from nervous agitation, restlessness, excessive sensitivity, and acute senses; as well as those who are easily excited and impressionable to pleasurable experiences that lead to overactivity of mind and body.

Rarely calm and collected, Coffea individuals are quick to act, full of ideas, and do everything with an anxious hastiness. Physically they seem to suffer from overacute hearing, excessive hunger, and sleeplessness, and they may exhibit a short, dry, nervous cough. Symptoms are worse from extreme emotions (pleasure), strong odors, noise, open air, cold, and at night. Warmth and lying down improve symptoms.

Conium maculatum (Poison Hemlock)

Mentally depressed, morose, timid, averse to company, and afraid of being alone, Conium individuals have suffered a great emotional trauma that leads to depression. They have no interest in any daily activities and seem unable to sustain any mental endeavor. Physically uncoordinated, Conium types exhibit a sudden lack of strength when walking as well as a labored gait, trembling, and stiffness of the legs. Stools may be hard and painful with frequent urging, followed by tremors and weakness after every evacuation. All symptoms are worse from any effort (mental or physical), lying down, or turning in or rising from bed. Missing a meal, being in the dark, letting the legs hang down, motion, and pressure all relieve symptoms.

Crocus sativus (Saffron)

Sudden changes in emotions—happiness and affection turning to anger, or cheerfulness suddenly changing to depression and sadness—call for this remedy. Crocus individuals may exhibit remorse over their poor behavior by lashing out, but are otherwise drowsy and fatigued. The eyes may be dry and burning, as though exposed to cool wind, and they often blink or hold them tightly closed. Symptoms are worse when lying down, during hot weather, or when confined to a warm room; in the morning, after having missed a meal, and before breakfast. Relief of symptoms occurs when in the open air.

Cuprum metallicum (Copper)

Individuals who have been exposed to violent situations and have experienced extreme fright that results in irregular, spasmodic, involuntary movements of the limbs or facial muscles, or even convulsions, will be greatly helped by this remedy. Aside from being frightened, these individuals also seem very ill-natured, almost malicious in their interactions with others. When physical pain is present (abdominal and intestinal distress), all pains are increased by movement and touch. All symptoms are worse in general from touch and after vomiting and are relieved by drinking cold water.

Gelsemium sempervirens (Yellow Jasmine)

The classic picture of stage fright: paralyzed with fear or limp with fright; prostrate, dizzy, drowsy, and trembling. Dull, weak, and listless with a desire to be left alone, Gelsemium individuals have suffered such an emotional shock that they are unable to sustain the level of fear expressed and simply can no longer react; they go limp and cease to move. Such high exposure to extreme emotional trauma leads to a variety of physical symptoms ranging from tea- or cream-colored diarrhea, profuse or retained urination, slowed respiration with great prostration, loss of muscular control or cramps in arms, and fevers with chills and tremors so violent they want to be held. All symptoms are worse in damp or foggy weather, before a thunderstorm, and at ten in the morning. Improvement from symptoms is seen when the individual bends forward, urinates profusely, is in the open air, and sustains continued motion.

Graphites (Plumbago [Black Lead])

Emotionally, Graphites individuals are easily startled, timid, indecisive, and disinclined to any effort; fidgety, apprehensive, and despondent. But Graphites works best in those individuals who are stout, fair, fat, and chilly with a tendency to skin afflictions and constipation. These individuals are insolent, teasing, and do not take correcting seriously. Skin symptoms of Graphites are most prominent and take two forms: rough, hard, cracked, and persistently dry; or spotted with eruptions or rawness in folds of skin, bends of limbs, groin, neck, or behind ears; all discharges are fluid, thin, and sticky. Symptoms (especially skin) are worse at night, from warmth, and better from being wrapped up.

Helleborus niger (Christmas Rose)

The symptoms of Helleborus are hallmarked by general muscular weakness attended by imperfect recognition of external sensations (hearing, vision, and taste distorted) and lack of ability to communicate with the outside world. These individuals are slow in responding to commands, voices, or stimuli; seem mentally blank and stare into space with much involuntary sighing; and appear completely withdrawn into a fantasy world. They may absently pick at the lips or bedding and exhibit every characteristic of depressed vitality. Although they seem totally motionless, there is an odd automatic motion of one arm and leg. Symptoms are always worse throughout the night from evening until morning and better from attention.

Hepar sulphuris calcareum (Hahnemann's Calcium Sulphide)

Hepar sulphuris calcareum individuals exhibit the highest degree of anger; touchy and hasty both mentally and physically; anger is so quick as to do great physical harm to others and is usually violent, explosive, and unpredictable. Other times Hepar individuals can be generally calm and peaceful but will manifest explosive anger if not understood by others. They are very frustrated from not being understood, and the slightest thing will irritate them. Hepar types also experience anguish in the evening and at night, with an obvious disinterest in living; they may also appear dejected and sad. Hepar is well suited to individuals with a tendency to skin eruptions and swollen glands, or with abscess formation with copious pussy discharges with a foul odor. All Hepar symptoms are made worse from cold, dry winds; cool air or the slightest draft; touch; and lying on the painful side. Improvement of Hepar symptoms is seen when the individual is warm, during damp weather, and from eating.

Hyoscyamus niger (Henbane)

Hyoscyamus individuals present a shocking picture of emotional derangement caused by emotional upset or trauma. Emotional shock has affected the nervous system so profoundly that it seems as though an evil entity has taken possession. They are suspicious, talkative, sexually obscene, jealous, fearful, and foolish. Tremulous weakness, spasms, and twitching of tendons may be seen, along with nervous agitation. The individual may suffer from sleeplessness with a tendency to jump up frightened. All symptoms are worse at night, after eating, and when lying down; and better from stooping.

Ignatia amara (St. Ignatius Bean)

These individuals are rash and abrupt with shallow emotions; prone to hysterical anger that dissipates quickly but leaves physical symptoms (diarrhea or painful passing of stools) in its wake. They have episodes of simultaneous multiple emotional states: weeping, laughter, and anger. Ignatia is useful in instances of profound grief that lingers and dulls normally enjoyed activities. Depressed, sad, and tearful; reluctant to relate to others; sighing and sobbing. Useful after shocks, grief, and disappointment. The sleep symptoms of Ignatia are most characteristic: sleep is light, and the limbs may jerk when falling asleep; there may be insomnia from grief or worry with itchiness of the forelimbs and excessive yawning. Ignatia symptoms are always worse in the morning, in open air, after eating, and from external warmth. Relief from symptoms is seen while eating and from a change of position.

Kali carbonicum (Carbonate of Potassium)

Characterized by alternating moods: despondent and irritable, and fearful and anxious, yet does not like to be left alone; never quiet or content; stubborn and oversensitive to pain, touch, and noise; strong and controlled to the point that the emotions are blocked. Suppressed emotions lead to abdominal tightness and cramping, with abdomen being cold and distended; experiences difficulty during defecation. Kali carbonicum is a most difficult individual. Weakness characterizes all complaints—emotional, constitutional, and physical: there is always a soft pulse, coldness, and lack of reaction. Disgust for all food except sweets. Symptoms are worse in cold weather, at three in the morning, and from lying on the left side. Improve-ment is noted during warm, moist weather; during the day; and when moving around.

Lac canium (Dog's Milk)

This is a very good remedy for nursing mothers of all species who lack an interest in newborn young, whether one out of the litter has died at birth or not. The emotional picture of Lac canium is forgetful, despondent with attacks of rage, and lacking in self-esteem. In all complaints there is a decided weakness and prostration, and symptoms are worse on the morning of one day and the evening of the next day. Symptoms are relieved from cold and cold drinks.

Lachesis (Bushmaster)

Despondent and sad, with no desire to be bothered with anyone or anything, Lachesis individuals are at their height of difficulty first thing in the morning. They are morose, restless, and uneasy; jealous and suspicious; and want to be off somewhere all the time. They may exhibit mental delirium and trembling. Classically known as a left-sided remedy since most of Lachesis symptoms tend to be on the left side of the body. These individuals are some of the most difficult to cope with. They may suffer from a tickling cough, which is worse when the throat is touched, and experience chronic constipation. Lachesis symptoms come on during sleep, and all symptoms are worse after sleep, in spring, from warm baths, and from pressure. Relief of Lachesis symptoms comes with the appearance of discharges (tears, menses, runny nose), and from warm applications.

Lilium tigrinum (Tiger Lily)

The remedy made from the tiger lily presents a most unusual array of mental and emotional symptoms. Usually female, these individuals display profound depression to the degree of apparent torment, coupled with an aggravation of emotional symptoms when consoled. There is a constant inclination to be weepy and morose, yet they are driven by a constant need to be busy in an aimless and hurried fashion. They may also be anxious and fearful, emotions that may escalate into striking out in anger.

Physical symptoms center primarily on the female reproductive and pelvic organs: with pain, acrid vaginal discharges, and a need to have the abdomen supported by resting it on the floor or furniture. There may be a constant desire to void the bowels, especially in early morning, accompanied by a hurried urgency; loose stools may also be present, with mucus and blood and much pain. All symptoms are worse from consolation and in a warm room and are better when exposed to fresh air. This remedy is slow to work, and good results are more often seen when used in medium to high potencies (30c to 200c); it should not be repeated too frequently, however, but be given time to work.

Lycopodium (Club Moss)

Lycopodium exhibits anger with cowardice. Usually male, Lycopodium individuals are intolerant of contradiction but lack self-confidence, so they won't argue the point because they feel vulnerable in confrontations. Feelings of vulnerability are often expressed as a fear of being alone. They are annoyed by very small things, apprehensive and reluctant to try new things. This is also a remedy that is well suited to young individuals who antagonize weaker or less intelligent playmates; in their own territories, these individuals can be bullies or dictators. Lycopodium individuals are especially irritable in the morning and often have complaints that develop slowly over time; difficulty with digestion is common, and characteristically, they have symptoms that progress from the right to the left side of the body. All symptoms are worse from about four in the afternon to eight in the evening and from heat and hot air. Emotional symptoms are worse in the morning. Symptoms improve after midnight and from motion, warm food and drink, and cold.

Lyssin or Hydrophobinum (Saliva of Rabid Dog)

This remedy acts primarily on the nervous system. There is great fear and sensitivity to all external stimuli. Shiny glittery objects and reflected sulight (as from light reflected off the surface of water) cause confusion and may even bring on convulsions. Fear escalates into uncontrollable rage with overt aggression; outbursts may be followed by a show of remorse or self-loathing or loss of self-trust. These individuals seek out dark places and shun company; it is difficult to trust such an unpredictable emotional state, and they themselves seem to understand that they cannot trust themselves. Physical symptoms vary: excessive sexual impulses; drooling; constant desire to swallow, with gagging when attempting to drink; an urge to defecate or urinate when seeing running water; watery stools that are profuse and worse in the evening. All symptoms are worse from the sight or sound of running water, glittering or reflected light, and the heat of the sun. Nothing relieves the symptoms. This remedy is available only with a prescription from a licensed veterinarian; consult your practitioner.

Mercurius vivus (Quicksilver)

Having loss of willpower and weary of life, Mercurius individuals seem slow, dull, and mistrustful. They may exhibit explosive and sudden anger, but it is short-lived. Physically, the glands, bones, and mucous membranes are all affected, to varying degrees, with abscesses, rheumatoid pains, and respiratory symptoms (cough with yellow expectoration being the most notable). The skin of a Mercurius individual is almost constantly moist, and they are usually sweaty and itchy. All symptoms are worse at night, during wet weather, from lying on the right side, from perspiring, in a warm room, and if too warm in bed. No events or conditions bring relief to Mercurius symptoms.

Natrum carbonicum (Carbonate of Sodium)

All remedies made from sodium stimulate the activity of cells, increasing their ability to utilize oxygen and metabolize raw material. Natrum carbonicum individuals find thinking and comprehension difficult. They are often depressed and worried. Their extreme sensitivity to noise, cold, and change of weather is exemplified by their anxiety and restlessness during thunderstorms or from hearing music. Other times they are spontaneously happy and gay, but this respite is short-lived, and soon they turn slow, depressed, and worried again. Physically, they are prone to constant clearing of the throat, have a weak digestion that is upset by the smallest change of diet, and have weak ankles that turn easily. All symptoms are worse when sitting, during thunderstorms and music, from the heat of summer, small drafts of cold air, changes in weather, and from direct sunlight. Moving around and rubbing the ears and nose all bring relief of symptoms.

Natrum muriaticum (Chloride of Sodium)

Natrum muriaticum is indicated when loss is experienced as an emotionally traumatic event, such as a violent accident. Withholds feelings of sadness or anger and has passionate outbursts when alone. These individuals stay in contact and observe others, but they themselves are emotionally isolated loners who do not allow others to help them and are worse for consolation. They misperceive the reality of a situation and maximize slight hurts; nurse old emotional injuries and seem to take a perverse delight in doing so. Miserable, dejected, rejected, and pitiful, they take great pleasure in instilling guilt in caregivers: "I'm miserable, and it's all your fault; if you loved me you'd do something (even if it means holding me in your lap all day)." Natrum muriaticum individuals may exhibit digestive symptoms: constipation alternating with diarrhea; stomach upsets, including vomiting of stomach acid; excessive thirst or lack of thirst; and unnatural hunger alternating with loss of appetite. Other symptoms may include chilliness as well as dry, itchy skin with scratching and chewing. Natrum muriaticum's emotional symptoms may be confused with those of Ignatia, but differentiation lies in the root experience: Ignatia grieves loss, Natrum muriaticum experiences the actual event as a trauma. Symptoms tend to be worse from the heat of the sun and summer weather, emotional stress, exertion of any kind, from consolation or sympathy, and on alternate days. Open air, cool bathing, sweating, rest, deep breaths, and going without regular meals all relieve symptoms.

Natrum phosphoricum (Phosphate of Sodium)

Natrum phosphoricum individuals are fearful, sharing with Phosphorus individuals an almost clairvoyant nature; they think that inanimate objects are people (or other animals) and will bark or shy away from them in fear. This is especially true at night, when they wake from sleep and fears overtake them. One pupil may look dilated (in Belladonna both are dilated), and there may be burping, sour vomiting, and greenish diarrhea. Sometimes these individuals will have hives or itchy skin—especially on the ankles. Like those of many other remedies, Natrum phosphoricum symptoms are worse during a thunderstorm, from drinking milk, and eating sugar. All forms of cold bring relief of symptoms.

Nitricum acidum (Nitric acid)

Hateful, irritable, spiteful, and stubborn on the surface, the underlying root of the emotional symptoms of this remedy is hopeless despair. These individuals are sensitive to noise, pain, touch, and movement and often fear that they will die. As with Calcarea carbonica and Cicuta, there is a desire to eat undigestible things (chalk or dirt), and their hunger is insatiable for any and all things. They especially crave salt and fats. A keynote symptom indicating this remedy is that the tissues of the outlets of the body, where mucous membrane and skin meet, are often affected with bleeding warts or ulcers. All symptoms are worse in the evening and at night, in a cold climate, and in hot weather. Relief of symptoms comes when riding in a car or with sustained rhythmic movement.

Nux vomica (Poison Nut)

The most irritable, with volcanic eruptions of anger (compare Hepar). Nux types are especially angry when interrupted; they feel burdened, hasty, and hurried. They are impatient with others and can be quarrelsome. They express anger openly and may get so angry as to tremble. These individuals are impossible to please; fastidious (compare Arsenicum album); difficult to live with and exhibit a crankiness that erupts (more slowly than Hepar) into violent anger. They may also be impatient and ambitious, and if interrupted will become angry. The typical Nux is characterized as cranky, crabby, slow, and sluggish; this individual is thin, dark, and can act edgy and nervous when exhaustion gets too great. All physical symptoms point to a physiology that is overwrought and overworked. Digestive troubles, nervous cough, constipation (or alternating with diarrhea), restless sleep after three in the morning—all point to a state of exhaustion. Everything is worse in the morning, after eating, from dry weather, touch, and anything cold. Relief comes from a brief nap, if allowed to finish it, and in damp, wet weather.

Phosphoricum acidum (Phosphoric acid)

Mental debility occurs first in these individuals, followed by physical debility, and this is a remedy that is excellent for those suffering from excess grief, acute disease, and loss of essential bodily fluids. Extreme apathy and indifference hallmark this remedy's emotional symptoms, along with listlessness, difficulty thinking, loss of awareness, and despair. Mental and emotional symptoms eventually give way to physical ones: intestinal gas, altered blood sugar counts, lack of or malabsorption of vitamin C leading to bone deformity. Individuals most susceptible to these symptoms generally grow too rapidly as youths and as adults become overworked either physically or mentally. All symptoms are worse from any activity, being spoken to, loss of essential body fluids, and restriction of circulation and better from keeping warm.

Phosphorus (Phosphorus)

Mentally, the Phosphorus individual is restless, fidgety, extrasensitive, and indifferent to being calmed. Easily startled or bothered by thunderstorms (or sudden, loud noises) and profoundly depressed, these individuals are also seen to be extremely fearful, as if something might pop out of no-where and get them. Physically, an underlying inflammatory and destructive process can be seen occurring throughout many body systems: mucous membranes, bones, blood, and hemorrhages throughout the body. Stools may be affected, appearing either white and hard, or as painless, abundant diarrhea. Respiratory symptoms include a hard, dry cough that causes the whole body to shake with each episode, and hoarseness or actual loss of voice. All symptoms are worse from touch, physical or mental activity, at twilight and during the evening, from warm food or drink, during a change of weather or thunderstorm, from getting wet in hot weather, and going up stairs. Symptoms improve in the dark, from eating cold food, in the open air, from bathing in cold water, and from sleeping.

Platina (Metallic Platinum)

In contrast to Phosphoric acid, the physical symptoms of Platina develop before mental ones, and physical symptoms disappear as mental symptoms develop. Numbness and coldness are keynote symptoms indicating this remedy, especially in the thighs, where there is the sensation that they are tightly wrapped; this causes the individual to sleep with the legs spread far apart for relief or to have difficulty standing or sitting up, owing to a feeling of weariness in the legs. Gas builds up in the digestive tract causing flatulence and a feeling of constriction, yet the appetite is ravenous. In females excessive sexual activity exists concurrent with depression or sadness; this is why this remedy is more frequently used for females than males. Physical symptoms give way as mental symptoms develop: arrogant, proud, and contemptuous of others, individuals may have an overdeveloped sense of self-importance or an irresistible impulse to kill someone or something; conversely, individuals may seem annoyed, dissatisfied, and exhausted. All symptoms are worse from standing or sitting up and during the evening; they are better when and from walking.

Psorinum (Scabies Vesicle)

The mental state of Psorinum is that of hopeless despair with profound and lingering depression. Skin symptoms usually accompany this remedy's list of symptoms: frantic itching of dry skin with dry, dull, rough hair. There may be small pimplelike eruptions on the skin, especially in the bends of the joints, which itch and are worse when the individual is warm. Although the hair is very dry and rough, the oil glands secrete excessive amounts of sebaceous fluid causing the skin to be excessively oily and have a dirty smell. Ulcers, eczema around the ears, and crusty eruptions all over (with an offensive odor) are general skin symptoms covered by this remedy. These individuals have an extreme sensitivity to cold in all forms, wanting to be kept very warm (wrapped up) even in the summer. Great physical debility also accompanies this remedy's symptoms, even in the absence of a physical disease or in cases in which the disease is no longer present, yet the individual remains weak and exhausted. All symptoms are worse from changes in weather, in hot sunshine, and cold in any form (there is a dread of even small drafts of cold air). Improvement is seen from heat in any form and from being wrapped up (even in summer), except when eruptions are present, in which case the heat will make them itch more. Psorinum is available only through a licensed veterinarian; consult your practitioner.

Pulsatilla (Wind Flower)

This remedy is indicated for individuals with a mild, yielding disposition who avoid getting angry. Mental symptoms are sometimes accompanied by upper and lower respiratory symptoms that have characteristic bland yellow or white mucus. These individuals are timid and lack self-confidence; they are fearful of being alone, especially in the evening; they like sympathy, being fussed over, and being caressed. Acutely overemotional, the mental state of Pulsatilla has been compared to an April day: gray and then suddenly almost cheerful, constantly shifting for brief periods from one mental state to another. The variability of Pulsatilla's emotional symptoms also extends to the physical symptoms of this remedy: no two stools are alike, even during the course of a day; heat in one part of the body, coldness in another; wide awake in the evening with extreme sleepiness in the afternoon; thirstlessness in nearly all situations; vomiting and stomach pains with ravenous hunger. All symptoms are worse from heat or in a warm room, from rich food and after eating, and in the evening. Symptoms are improved in the open air, during motion, from eating cold food, drinking cold water (although not thirsty), or when cold water is applied to the body. Pulsatilla is the chronic remedy for Natrum muriaticum individuals: when a constitutionally Natrum muriaticum individual becomes acutely ill, he or she will often respond to Pulsatilla.

Rhododendron chrysanthum (Yellow Snow Rose)

Like Phosphorus, these individuals are very afraid of thunderstorms, and dread their approach. They are also forgetful. A true guiding physical symptom of this remedy is that all symptoms are worse just before a storm; when accompanied by rheumatic symptoms and symptoms of gout, there is a clear indication for using this remedy. The neck may be stiff, and the joints are often swollen with tearing pains in the limbs, especially on the right side, which are worse during rest and when resting; bone pains reappear after a change of weather; and sleep is always with the legs crossed. All symptoms are worse before a storm, at night and toward morning, and *always* reappear in harsh weather. Relief of symptoms occurs after the storm breaks, with warmth, and from eating.

Rhus toxicodendron (Poison Ivy)

Mentally, Rhus presents the type that is listless and sad with a small mixture of slight fearfulness during the day. Fearfulness and anxiety increase with the onset of night and escalate to the point that this individual cannot remain in bed. When these mental symptoms combine with the physical symptoms of extreme restlessness with constant shift of position, rheumatic pains that are improved from stretching out the limbs, itchy skin, sneezing, and diarrhea, this remedy is effective. Two keynote symptoms of Rhus are a tongue coated white except for a triangular patch of red at the tip and stiffness when rising that is relieved when the individual limbers up after movement. All symptoms are worse during sleep, in wet, rainy weather and after rain, at night, and while resting. Symptoms will be relieved from being warmed, during dry weather, from limbering up, walking, motion or a change of position, stretching out the limbs, and warm baths.

Sepia (Inky Juice of Cuttlefish)

Sepia types are unable to love or emotionally connect with others, and when approached, their irritability pours out. They don't want to be needed, feel emotionally bankrupt (except for peevishness), and are very indifferent to other family members or to activities. Sepia individuals can also be snappish when touched, approached, or spoken to, but their testiness stops as soon as attention is withdrawn, and they are left alone. Frequently a female remedy owing to the many symptoms of the female reproductive tract: a bearing-down sensation in the lower abdomen as if everything might fall out; greenish yellow vaginal discharges; and prolapse of uterus. General physical symptoms of Sepia include weakness, a yellowish complexion, and chilliness with shivering and thirst; the latter two of which are worse toward evening. Symptoms are typically worse in the evenings and before noon, from warm baths, dampness, in cold air, and before a thunderstorm. Symptoms are improved by exercise, pressure, warmth, hot compresses, drawing up the limbs, cold baths, and after sleep.

Silicea (Silica, Pure Flint)

Submissive, cowardly, and anxious, Silicea individuals are nervous and excitable with an extreme sensitivity to all impressions because they are exhausted mentally and emotionally. They can also be bullheaded and unreasonable, which shows when they get fixed ideas and will not be distracted from them. This is one of the "colder remedies"; these individuals must have warmth: they hug the fire or heater and will not tolerate cold in any form; their feet are cold; they hate cold drafts of any kind; all symptoms of intolerance to cold are much worse in winter. Too, they are prone to wet, watery head colds with lots of watery sneezing, especially in the morning. Mucus will dry on the nose leaving crusty patches, or sneezing may be so violent as to cause nosebleeds. Often, there is a history of chronic abscesses with much pus formation or upper respiratory disease. All symptoms are worse from dampness and cold and are improved from warmth, in the summer, and during wet, humid weather.

Staphysagria (Stavesacre)

Staphysagria is a helpful remedy when loss is accompanied by anger that has a component of a deep sense of injustice or betrayal. Characterized by suppressed emotions and swallowed pride; usually sweet and vulnerable, unassertive and nonaggressive. They will go to any length to avoid hurting others and are afraid to demonstrate anger. When provoked, they will not express anger directly but will later direct temper tantrums at objects, rather than at people or family members to which they are loyal and defending. May be accompanied by a history of oppression. Prefers solitude and is peevish; wants things but refuses them when offered (compare Chamomilla). Teeth may be loose, aching, decayed, and crumbling. Symptoms are worse from experiencing unpleasant emotions, touch, cold drinks, stretching the limbs, and at night. Warmth, rest, and eating breakfast all relieve symptoms.

Stramonium (Thorn Apple)

The mental and emotional symptoms of this remedy are similar to those of Belladonna and Lyssin. With a constant desire to communicate with others, Stramonium individuals assume a very animated manner that incorporates the entire array of emotions; rapid changes from joy to sadness; violence and lewdness; derangement and distraction. These individuals cannot bear to be alone and are unable to tolerate darkness. They always seek light and company, but when approached, they will attempt to escape.

As with Lyssin, the sight of water or anything glittering may bring on spasms. Likewise, there is an aversion to water accompanied by spasms in the throat, which may look like a chewing motion of the jaws, and frequently, there is a loss of the voice. The eyes look prominent and widely staring with dilated pupils but lack the glitter of Belladonna. The face is hot, red, and distorted and may have an expression of terror. Usually, Stramonium individuals are very sleepy but cannot sleep; if they do sleep, they awake in terror, sometimes screaming in fright. Spasms in the legs may cause graceful rhythmic motions, trembling, twitching of tendons, or a staggering gait. All symptoms are worse in a dark room, when alone, looking at shiny or bright objects, after sleep, and when swallowing. Symptoms are better in bright light, from the company of others, and from warmth.

Sulphur (Sublimated Sulphur)

Sulphur is especially appropriate for older subjects who manifest childish anger or peevishness at small offenses. When offered affection, they respond to the gesture with annoyance: "You're bothering/smothering/interrupting me." They tend to be very ill-tempered, irritable, and selfish with no regard for others. Physically, the body may give off actual heat and appear itchy when angry; the breath, skin, and all body fluids smell sour and foul. These itchy-scratchy individuals have been referred to as the great unwashed and the great unwashable; no matter how frequently they are bathed or how clean their environment, they always appear and smell dirty. Often they are gaunt and lacking in body tone, even when they have a good appetite. They are prone to attacks of painless morning diarrhea, which occurs on waking and must be attended to with great haste. All symptoms are worse when at rest, when standing, from being warm, from bathing, in the morning and at night, and periodically (occurring with regularity in a specific season or hour of the day). Relief of symptoms occurs in warm, dry weather.

Veratrum album (White Hellebore)

The physical symptoms of Veratrum are often the result of becoming frightened. These individuals experience a great deal of violent, cramping physical pain, which causes them to have disagreeable emotional symptoms. Argumentative, cross and quarrelsome, and irrational or mentally wandering, Veratrum individuals may also exhibit deep depression and sit in silence for long periods. This is a thirsty individual, who craves ice water or sour drinks, but experiences violent cramping and immediate nausea and vomiting when eating or drinking even the smallest amounts. Frothy vomiting is immediately followed by colicky cramps in the legs and collapse, with the body icy cold.

The face is pale, frowning, and distorted with a terrified look, and the tongue is remarkable in appearance: it appears white or yellow with a red stripe down the middle. Twitching and convulsions of face and legs are frequently seen—in the legs this is caused by severe pain in the joints and electric-like shocks—and is often accompanied by a fever. Diarrhea is frequent, watery, green or colorless, and odorless. All symptoms are especially worse from physical activity and drinking or eating, and moderately worse from cold drinks, during an attack of pain, in cold, wet weather, and from fright. Relief from symptoms is found from hot drinks, walking around, being covered, and lying down.

Nonhomeopathic Aids to Emotional Symptoms

Nature's Rescue (A Bach Flower Preparation)

Contains the following ingredients in an alcohol-based tincture: *Helianthemum nummularium, Clematis vitalba, Impatiens glandulifera, Prunus cerasifera,* and *Ornithogalum umbellatum.* Symptoms for use include any emotional and psychological stress. Although the Bach brand Nature's Rescue contains an extract from one of the Clematis species flowers, it may safely be used for rabbits. The species of Clematis used is not poisonous to rabbits; I have used this Bach flower essence safely—and with good results—with several rabbits on more than one occasion.

Broken Heart Remedy

A special recipe made by Deb Soule of Avena Botanicals, which contains a combination of hawthorn flowers and berries, motherwort, lemon balm, heartsease pansy, and flower essences of hawthorn and heartsease pansy. Indications for use include loss, grief, and bereavement.

Remedies Used in This Book

ABBREVIATION	REMEDY	ORIGIN
Acon	Aconitum napellus	Monkshood
Am c	Ammonium carbonicum	Carbonate of Ammonia
Apis	Apis mellifica	Honeybee
Arg n	Argentum nitricum	Nitrate of Silver
Arn	Arnica montana	Leopard's Bane
Ars	Arsenicum album	Arsenic Trioxide
Aur	Aurum metallicum	Metallic Gold
Bar c	Baryta carbonica	Carbonate of Baryta
Bell	Belladonna	Deadly Nightshade
Bor	Borax	Borate of Sodium
Bry	Bryonia	Wild Hops
Calc	Calcarea carbonica	Carbonate of Lime
Camph	Camphora	Camphor
Canth	Cantharis	Spanish Fly

ABBREVIATION	REMEDY	ORIGIN
Caps	Capsicum	Cayenne Pepper
Carb an	Carbo animalis	Animal Charcoal
Carb v	Carbo vegetabilis	Vegetable Charcoal
Cham	Chamomilla	German Chamomile
Cic	Cicuta virosa	Water Hemlock
Cina	Cina	Worm Seed
Coff	Coffea cruda	Unroasted Coffee
Con	Conium maculatum	Poison Hemlock
Croc	Crocus sativus	Saffron
Cupr	Cuprum metallicum	Copper
Gels	Gelsemium sempervirens	Yellow Jasmine
Graph	Graphites	Plumbago (Black Lead)
Hell	Helleborus niger	Christmas Rose
Hep	Hepar sulphuris calcareum	Hahnemann's Calcium Sulphide
Hyos	Hyoscyamus niger	Henbane
Ign	Ignatia amara	St. Ignatius Bean
Kali c	Kali carbonicum	Carbonate of Potassium
Lac c	Lac canium	Dog's Milk
Lach	Lachesis	Bushmaster
Lil t	Lilium tigrinum	Tiger Lily
Lyc	Lycopodium	Club Moss
Lyss	Lyssin (Hydrophobinum)	Saliva of Rabid Dog
Merc	Mercurius vivus	Quicksilver
Nat c	Natrum carbonicum	Carbonate of Sodium
Nat m	Natrum muriaticum	Chloride of Sodium
Nat p	Natrum phosphoricum	Phosphate of Sodium

ABBREVIATION	REMEDY	ORIGIN
Nit ac	Nitricum acidum	Nitric Acid
Nux v	Nux vomica	Poison Nut
Ph ac	Phosphoricum acidum	Phosphoric Acid
Phos	Phosphorus	Phosphorus
Plat	Platina	Metallic Platinum
Psor	Psorinum	Scabies Vesicle
Puls	Pulsatilla	Wind Flower
Rhod	Rhododendron chrysanthum	Yellow Snow Rose
Rhus t	Rhus toxicodendron	Poison Ivy
Sep	Sepia	Inky Juice of Cuttlefish
Sil	Silicea	Silica, Pure Flint
Staph	Staphysagria	Stavesacre
Stram	Stramonium	Thorn Apple
Sulph	Sulphur	Sublimated Sulphur
Verat	Veratrum album	White Hellebore

Further Reading

BOOKS

Bright, Michael. *Barks, Roars and Siren Songs: How Animals Talk to Us and How We Talk Back.* New York: Carol Publishing Group, 1991.

Chappell, Peter. *Emotional Healing with Homeopathy: A Self-help Manual.* Rockport, Mass.: Element Books, 1995.

Cohen, Barbara and Louise Taylor. *Cats and Their Women.* Boston: Little, Brown and Co., 1992.

———. *Dogs and Their Women.* Boston: Little, Brown and Co., 1989.

Coleman, Joan. *Forever Friends. Resolving Conflict and Grief After the Loss of a Beloved Animal.* Las Vegas, N.V.: J. C. Tara Enterprises, 1993.

Coren, Stanley. *The Intelligence of Dogs: A Guide to the Thoughts, Emotions and Inner Lives of Our Canine Companions.* New York: Bantam Books, 1995.

Corey, Paul. *Do Cats Think? Notes of a Cat Watcher.* Chicago: Regnery, 1977.

Dodman, Nicholas. *The Dog Who Loved Too Much: Tales, Treatment and the Psychology of Dogs.* New York: Bantam Books, 1996.

Griffin, Donald R. *Animal Thinking.* Cambridge, Mass.: Harvard University Press, 1985.

Hedren, Tippi and Theodore Taylor. *The Cats Of Shambala.* Acton, Calif.: Tiger Island Press, 1992.

Lagoni, Laurel S. et al. *The Human-Animal Bond and Grief.* Philadelphia, Penn.: W. B. Saunders, 1994.

Lemiux, Christina M. *Coping with the Loss of a Pet: A Gentle Guide for All Who Love a Pet.* Reading, Penn.: Wallace R. Clark, 1989.

Martyn, Elizabeth and David Taylor. *The Little Cat Behavior Book.* New York: Dorling Kindersley, 1991.

Moussaieff, Jerry, Mason McCarthy, and Susan McCarthy. *When Elephants Weep: The Emotional Lives of Animals.* New York: Delecort Press, 1995.

Serpel, James. *In the Company of Animals.* New York: Cambridge University Press, 1996.

Smith, Penelope. *Animal Talk: Interspecies Telepathic Communication,* 3rd rev. ed. Point Reyes, Calif.: Pegasus Publications, 1989.

———. *Animals: Our Return to Wholeness.* Point Reyes, Calif.: Pegasus Publications, 1993.

Tellington-Jones, Linda. *The Telling Touch: A Breakthrough in Healing and Communication.* New York: Viking Penguin, 1992.

Thomas, Elizabeth Marshall. *The Hidden Life of Dogs.* New York: Houghton Mifflin Co., 1995.

———. *The Tribe of Tiger: Cats and Their Culture.* New York: Touchstone Books, 1995.

Wilson, Danny. *Curing Your Dog's Bad Habits: Treating Behavioral Problems.* New York: Sterling, 1993.

Wright, Machaelle Small. *Behaving As If the God in All Life Mattered: A New Age Ecology.* Warrenton, Va.: Perelandra, 1987.

NEWSLETTERS

The Animals' Advocate
A quarterly newsletter of
The Animal Legal Defense Fund
1363 Lincoln Avenue
San Rafael, CA 94901

MAGAZINES

Best Friends
Best Friends Animal Sanctuary
Kanab, UT 84741-5001
(801) 644-2001 (subscription)

Clubs and Organizations

American Society for the
Prevention of Cruelty to
Animals
441 East 92nd Street
New York, NY 10128
(212) 876-7700

Animal Legal Defense Fund
1363 Lincoln Avenue
San Rafael, CA 94901
(415) 459-0885

Association of Veterinarians
for Animal Rights
P.O. Box 6269
Vacaville, CA 95696
(707) 451-1391

Delta Society or
Pet Partners Program
321 Burnett Avenue South
Third Floor
Renton, WA 98055-02569
(206) 226-7357

Fund for Animals
200 West 57th Street
New York, NY 10019
(212) 246-2096

Greenpeace USA
1611 Connecticut Avenue, NW
Washington, DC 20009
(202) 462-1177

Humane Society of the United
States (HSUS)
2100 L Street, NW
Washington, DC 20037
(202) 452-1100

International Fund for
Animal Welfare
P.O. Box 193
Yarmouth Port, MA 02675
(877) 932-4329

International Society for
Animal Rights, Inc.
421 South State Street
Clarks Summit, PA 18411
(717) 586-2200

International Wildlife Coalition
1807 H Street, NW, Suite 301
Washington, DC 20006
(202) 347-0822

Interspecies Communication
273 Hidden Meadow Lane
Friday Harbor, WA 98250

People for the Ethical Treatment
of Animals (PETA)
P.O. Box 42516
Washington, DC 20015
(202) 726-0156

Progressive Animal Welfare
Society (PAWS)
P.O. Box 1037
Lynnwood, WA 98046
(206) 743-3845

Sources for Products

HOMEOPATHIC SUPPLIERS

Bailey's Pharmacy
175 Hartford Avenue
Allston, MA 02134
(617) 782-7202

Boiron
98C West Cochran Street
Simi Valley, CA 93065
(800) BLU-TUBE (258-8823)
(805) 582-9091
(805) 582-9094 (Fax)

Dolisos America
3014 Rigel Avenue
Las Vegas, NV 89102
(800) DOLISOS (635-4767)
(702) 871-9670 (Fax)

Hahnemann Medical
Clinic/Pharmacy
828 San Pablo Avenue
Albany, CA 94706
(510) 527-3003

Homeopathic Educational Services
2124 Kitteridge Street #N
Berkeley, CA 94704
(800) 359-9051 (orders only)
(510) 649-0294

Homeopathy Overnight
RR 1, Box 818
Kingfield, ME 04947
(800) ARNICA-3 (276-4223)
(207) 265-0029 (Fax)
http://www. somtel.com/
homeovernight

Luyties Pharmacal Company
4200 Laclede Avenue
St. Louis, MO 63108
(800) 325-8080

Merz Apothecary, Inc.
4716 North Lincoln Avenue
Chicago, IL 60625
(800) 252-0275
(312) 989-0900

Washington Homeopathic Products
4914 Del Ray Avenue
Bethesda, MD 20814
(800) 336-1695 (orders)
TDD available
(301) 656-1695
(301) 656-1847 (Fax)

HERBS AND FLOWER ESSENCES

Avena Botanicals Herbal Products
Avena Botanicals
20 Mill Street
Rockland, ME 04841
(207) 594-0694
(Broken Heart Remedy)

Nelson Bach USA
1007 West Upsal
Philadelphia, PA 19119
(800) 314-2224
(978) 958-0233 (Fax)
(Nature's Rescue or Calming Essence)

Notes

INTRODUCTION

1. See appendix 3 for addresses of these organizations.
2. Joseph Wylder, *Psychic Pets Secret Life* (Avenel, N.J.: Random House Value, 1995).
3. Nena Norton, personal telephone communication, June 7, 1994.
4. Elisabeth Kübler-Ross, *On Death and Dying* (New York: Macmillan, 1991).
5. The Pet Loss Support Hotline is a service provided by the Pet Loss Support Program at the College of Veterinary Medicine, Michigan State University, East Lansing, Michigan 48824. Phone: (517) 432-2696 (callers place calls at their own expense). Hours: 6:30 P.M.–9:30 P.M. Eastern Time on Tuesday, Wednesday, and Thursday. Established in 1994, this nonprofit program is funded by donations from individuals, veterinarians, veterinary associations, private foundations, and companion-animal related industries. Staffed by veterinary students trained by a professional grief counselor, the hotline

provides a nonjudgmental arena for people to express their feelings about companion animal loss; staff persons may also be able to assist callers with finding support in their local area.

CHAPTER 3

1. Konrad Lorenz, *The Year of The Greylag Goose,* trans. Robert Martin (New York: Harcourt Brace Jovanovich, 1978).
2. Konrad Lorenz, *Man Meets Dog* (New York: Penguin Books, 1988), 169.
3. Ibid.
4. The Delta Society or Pet Partners Program can be contacted at 321 Burnett Avenue South, Renton, Wash. 98055-02569; (206) 226-7357.
5. Richard Pitcairn and Susan Hubble Pitcairn, *Dr. Richard Pitcairn's Complete Guide to Natural Health For Dogs and Cats* (Emmaus, Penn.: Rodale Press, 1995), 147; Diane Stein, *Natural Healing For Dogs and Cats* (Freedom, Calif.: Crossing Press, 1993), 34.
6. Allen Boone, *Kinship With All Life* (San Francisco: Harper, 1954).
7. Lorenz, *Man Meets Dog,* 53.
8. Ibid., ix.
9. Elizabeth Marshall Thomas, *The Tribe of Tiger: Cats and Their Culture* (New York: Touchstone Books, 1995).

CHAPTER 4

1. Richard Adams, *Watership Down* (New York: Macmillan, 1974).

CHAPTER 6

1. Kübler-Ross, *On Death and Dying.*
2. Lorenz, *Man Meets Dog,* 194.

CHAPTER 7

1. William Boericke, *Pocket Manual of Homoeopathic Materia Medica* (ninth edition, 1927. Reprint, Santa Rosa, Calif.: Boericke and Tafel, 1982), 125.

CHAPTER 8

1. Nena Norton, personal telephone communication, April 5, 1995.
2. Pitcairn and Pitcairn, *Dr. Richard Pitcairn's Complete Guide to Natural Health For Dogs and Cats,* 146, 174–175.
3. Christopher Day, *The Homoeopathic Treatment of Small Animals: Principles and Practice* (New Delhi: B. Jain Publishers, 1984), 101.
4. Samuel Hahnemann, *The Organon of Medicine,* 9th ed. (New Delhi: B. Jain Publishers, 1990), 94–99.
5. George Macleod, *Cats: Homoeopathic Remedies* (Essex, England: C. W. Daniel Company, 1990), 1–2.
6. Day, *Homoeopathic Treatment of Small Animals,* 28, 34, 111–112.
7. George Macleod, *Cats: Homoeopathic Remedies,* 3.
8. Day, *The Homoeopathic Treatment of Small Animals,* 32–33.
9. Ibid., 33.
10. Diane Stein, *Natural Healing for Dogs and Cats,* 151.

CHAPTER 9

1. Boericke, *Homoeopathic Materia Medica,* 342.
2. Ibid., 460.
3. Ibid., 459.

CHAPTER 10

1. Lorenz, *Man Meets Dog,* 195.

Selected Bibliography

Barthel, Horst. *Synthetic Repertory: Psychic and General Symptoms of the Homoeopathic Materia Medica.* 3d ed. 3 vols. Heidelberg, Germany: Karl F. Haug Verlag, 1987.

Biddis, K. J., and George Macleod. *Homaeopathy in Veterinary Practice.* 2d. ed. Essex, England: C. W. Daniel Company, 1990.

Boericke, William. *Pocket Manual of Homoeopathic Materia Medica.* 9th ed., 1927. Philadelphia: Boericke and Tafel, 1982.

Boger, C. M. *A Synoptic Key to the Materia Medica (A Treatise for Homoeopathic Students).* 1921 Reprint, New Delhi, India: B. Jain Publishers, 1993.

Boone, J. Allen. *Kinship With All Life.* San Francisco: Harper, 1954.

Chapman, J. B., and J. W. Cogswell, eds. *Dr. Schuessler's Biochemistry: A Natural Method of Healing.* Northamptonshire, England: Thorsons Publishers, 1980.

Coulter, Catherine R. *Portraits of Homoeopathic Medicines: Psychophysical Analyses of Selected Constitutional Types.* 2 vols. Berkeley, Calif.: North Atlantic Books, 1986.

Day, Christopher. *The Homoeopathic Treatment of Small Animals: Principles and Practice.* New Delhi, India: B. Jain Publishers, 1988.

Dock, Lavinia L. *Text-Book of Materia Medica for Nurses.* New York and London: G. P. Putnam's Sons, 1912.

Farrington, E. A. *Clinical Materia Medica.* 1887. 4th ed., rev. New Delhi, India: B. Jain Publishers, 1992.

———. *Comparative Materia Medica.* New Delhi, India: B. Jain Publishers, 1991.

Gibson, Douglas. *Studies of Homoeopathic Remedies.* Edited by Marianne Harling and Brian Kaplan. Bucks, England: Beaconsfield Publishers, 1987.

Hahnemann, Samuel. *Organon of Medicine.* 1854. 6th ed. Translated by William Boericke. New Delhi, India: B. Jain Publishers, 1990.

Harndall, J. S. *Homoeopathy in Veterinary Practice.* 1989. Rev. ed. New Delhi, India: B. Jain Publishers, 1991.

Kent, James Tyler. *Repertory of the Homoeopathic Materia Medica and a Word Index.* London: Homoeopathic Book Service, 1986.

Klunker, Will. *Synthetic Repertory,* 3 vols. Heidelberg, Germany: Karl F. Haug Verlag, 1974.

Kübler-Ross, Elisabeth. *On Death and Dying.* New York: Macmillan, 1991.

Lazarus, Pat. *Keep Your Pet Healthy the Natural Way.* New Canaan, Ct.: Keats Publishing, 1983.

Leonard, Henri C. *The Pocket Materia Medica and Therapeutics.* 1886. 2d. ed. Detroit: The Illustrated Medical Journal Company, 1895.

Levine, Stephen. *Healing into Life and Death.* New York: Doubleday, 1987.

Lorenz, Konrad Z. *Man Meets Dog.* Translated by Marjorie K. Wilson, 1988. Reprint, New York: Kodansha, 1994.

Lorenz, Konrad Z. *The Year of the Greylag Goose.* Translated by Robert Martin. New York: Harcourt Brace Jovanovich, 1978.

Macleod, George. *Cats: Homoeopathic Remedies.* Essex, England: C. W. Daniel Company, 1990.

————. *A Veterinary Materia Medica and Clinical Repertory with a Materia Medica of the Nosodes.* Essex, England: C. W. Daniel Company, 1983.

Moore, James. *Dog Diseases Treated by Homoeopathy.* 1984. 7th ed. New Delhi, India: B. Jain Publishers, 1991.

Parent-Vriends, Lucia. *The New Rabbit Handbook.* New York: Barron's Educational Services, 1989.

Pitcairn, Richard, and Susan Hubble Pitcairn. *Dr. Richard Pitcairn's Complete Guide to Natural Health For Dogs and Cats.* Emmaus, Penn.: Rodale Press, 1995.

Ruddock, Edward H. *The Pocket Manual of Homoeopathic Veterinary Medicine: Containing the Symptoms, Causes, and Treatment of the Diseases of Horses, Cattle, Sheep, Swine, and Dogs.* 1984. 3d ed., rev. New Delhi, India: B. Jain Publishers, 1989.

Rush, John. *The Hand-Book to Veterinary Homoeopathy: or the Homoeopathic Treatment of the Horse, the Ox, the Sheep, the Dog, and the Swine.* 1984, 2d ed. New Delhi, India: B. Jain Publishers, 1990.

Stein, Diane. *Natural Healing for Dogs and Cats.* Freedom, Calif.: Crossing Press, 1993.

Thomas, Elizabeth Marshall. *The Tribe of Tiger: Cats and Their Culture.* New York: Touchstone Books, 1994.

Wolff, H. G. *Your Healthy Cat.* Berkeley: Homeopathic Book Services, 1991.

Wylder, Joseph. *Psychic Pets Secret Lives.* New York: Gramercy Books, 1978.

Acknowledgments

There are many people to thank for their participation in the writing of this book. To Nena Norton I am grateful for many forms of support, for her inspiration, her love, her lessons about the wonders of manifestation. I will miss her companions James, General, Pickles, and Frisky. Without her I would not have come to know Tushwa, who understands that I am perfect in my imperfection.

Because of Tom Prescott, Cat came into my life. She is a great joy to me. I know that Ernest keeps an eye on both of us, and I hope he is pleased with my efforts on her behalf.

In the early days, Bitsa Turner was my beacon on a dark horizon, presenting a third option I had not dared hope was possible. A turning point, she and the old gang at Drop-In made everything that followed within my reach.

Lisa Hawkins is due an award for friendship and caring well above and beyond the call of duty. She helped keep my household going, supplied boxes of tissues, and never let me give up. She helped me get home again to my beloved ocean, and mothered the motherless child in me.

Like her human companion, Wendy Kochenthal, I will miss Muffin. I am deeply inspired that Wendy lives the message I hope to impart in this book.

My thanks to my brother-in-law, Bill Collins, for keeping my car going, his sense of humor, and tires! And my sister, Karen, for loving me, praising me, and being my family.

I thank Cher Jones, Ed Barker, Kyle Aveni, and Cecil Gary for putting up with me on days when I wasn't fit company for man or paintbrush. (Kyle, I forgive you for leaving me stranded on the porch roof.)

The heart of what's in this book is exemplified by the life of my best true-blue friend, Kathleen Kravik. She puts her heart, love, soul, and endless tenderness into helping the strays of Waldo County, Maine. She has shared my joys and victories, and showed up at my house with lists of things for me to do, when things weren't going so smoothly. The only difficulty I ever have with her is that she's always right.

I am grateful to Bev and Albert Poliquin for giving Bruno the life he so much deserves, and for loving him (and putting up with him).

Jeannine Ann's artwork compliments this book. It was a joy to see her blossom as an artist and a human filled with Christ consciousness as she completed her contribution. Because of her efforts, I can share with you, dear reader, the lovely faces of these four-footed friends of mine.

Since our Goddard days, Diana Gould has stood beside me. As friend, advisor, and contemporary she has walked many paths with me. May she always walk in beauty.

Charlie Vellieux has walked The Good Red Road with me. To gatherings and teachings, he has been a protective and caring companion. His drumming keeps my spirit nourished as I write.

During the early drafts of this book Chris Sumner shared the story of her loss, gave encouragement, and extended a hand in friendship.

Many thanks and gratitude go to all the folks at Inner Traditions International. It all began with Jon Graham, who read the first draft and accepted the manuscript for publication. During the initial stages Deborah Kimbell was straightforward in a manner that made it possible for me to proceed with clarity and purpose. Rowan Jacobsen, my editor, slaved through my bad grammar, horrendous punctuation, poor sentence structure, and never once complained. If there is a patience award, he deserves it. I thank Peri Champine for her work on the cover design, Rachel Goldenberg for her lovely text design, and I owe a debt of gratitude to Jeff Euber and Kristi Tate for putting me and my work into the public arena. There are, of course, others who worked on different elements of the book who I also thank for bringing this beautiful book together so that I could share it with you.